Work Useful to Religion and the Humanities

Pickwick Studies in the History of Religion

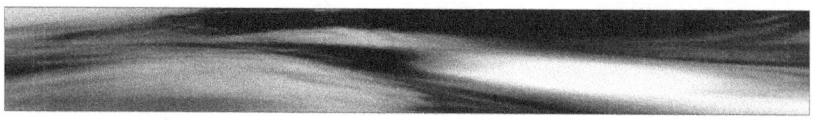

Series Editors
AMIR HUSSAIN and RICK TALBOTT

Work Useful to Religion and the Humanities

The Comparative Method in Religion from Las Casas to Tylor

Laura Ammon

⮞PICKWICK *Publications* • Eugene, Oregon

WORK USEFUL TO RELIGION AND THE HUMANITIES
The Comparative Method in Religion from Las Casas to Tylor

Pickwick Studies in the History of Religion 1

Copyright © 2012 Laura Ammon. All rights reserved. Except for brief quotations in critical publications or reviews, no part of this book may be reproduced in any manner without prior written permission from the publisher. Write: Permissions, Wipf and Stock Publishers, 199 W. 8th Ave., Suite 3, Eugene, OR 97401.

Pickwick Publications
A Division of Wipf and Stock Publishers
199 W. 8th Ave., Suite 3
Eugene, OR 97401

www.wipfandstock.com

ISBN 13: 978-1-60608-098-6

Cataloging-in-Publication data:

Ammon, Laura
   Work useful to religion and the humanities : the comparative method in religion from Las Casas to Tylor / Laura Ammon.

   Pickwick Studies in the History of Religion 1

   ISBN 13: 978-1-60608-098-6

   xii + 124 p. ; 23 cm. Includes bibliographical references.

   1. Religions—Historiography—History. 2. Religion—Study and Teaching—History. 3. Casas, Bartolomé de las, 1474–1566. 4. Sahagún, Bernardino de, d. 1590. 5. Acosta, José de, 11540–1600. 6. Lafitau, Joseph-François, 1681–1746. 7. Tylor, Edward Burnett, Sir, 1832–1917. I. Title. II. Series.

BL41 .A50 2012

Manufactured in the USA

To My Grandmother Marjorie Ammon

Contents

Acknowledgments | ix
List of Abbreviations | xi

1 Introduction | 1
2 The Comparative Method and Sacrifice in the New World | 22
3 The Comparative Method and Reflections of Antiquity | 56
4 The Comparative Method, Religion, and Civilization | 83
5 Conclusion | 112

Bibliography | 117

Acknowledgments

IT WOULD BE DIFFICULT for this tiny page of acknowledgments to adequately express the gratitude I feel toward all the people in my life who have been on this journey with me. I cannot let go of this study without giving credit to those people who make my world such a delightful place. Thank you from the bottom of my heart, all of you.

My students faithfully helped me hunt down articles and discussed readings with me. Gabriella Dattadeen, Paul Moore, Vicky Salim, and Ana Lee-Yee were all outstanding supporters and give me hope for the future.

My colleagues provided wonderful sounding boards and gentle guidance. Fay Bothom, Lynn Euzenas, and Joe Price always listened thoughtfully and asked provocative and helpful questions as I worked through the details of the project. I know it is a stronger book because of their help.

My support network of friends and family eased the way and offered support, encouragement, and the right combination of shoring-up and nudging to keep me on track through the past few years. Shannon Beets, Mark Cronan, Meg Garrett, Sandy Hereld, Sammie McGlasson, Melody Mooney, Karen Torjesen, and Glenn Yocum—I cannot thank you enough for your love and friendship. I would have been lost without you. And, in the I'd-be-lost-without-you category, Nana Sadamura provided coaching and an steadfast shoulder for me to lean on as I worked out the contours of my argument and my life.

I am indebted to my committee for their kindness and their thoughtful guidance. Ken Wolf offered insight and support, especially at the beginning of the project, and I am very grateful for his time and help. Lori Anne Ferrell provided comfort and consolation through long days of writer's block as well as a strong line edit that made this dissertation much stronger. Ann Taves offered vision and clarity when I could not see the path clearly and

Acknowledgments

gave me the tools to write this project. This project has benefitted tremendously from the patience and support of the editors and staff at Pickwick Publications.

My partner, Randy Reed, makes everything in life so much better. His careful attention to my work and his unwavering support made the entire endeavor possible. He has been an unfaltering companion and a comfort day and night. There is no way this would be possible without his kind and generous presence in my life.

Abbreviations

Brevisma	*Brevísma relación de la destrucción de las Indias*
FC	Florentine Codex
Moeurs	*Moeurs des sauvages américains comparées aux moeurs des premiers temps*
PC	Primitive Culture

1

Introduction

What I have given here is only a very imperfect sketch of what can be done. Still it contains a plan on which work useful to religion and the humanities can be done . . . I protest that I shall be infinitely obliged to any who may wish to correct me on any points where I may have misunderstood or gone astray, or furnish new proofs on which to base my conjectures or to make new ones.

JOSEPH-FRANCOIS LAFITAU
Moeurs des Sauvages Ameriquains

THE GREAT VARIETY OF peoples and cultures of the New World offered unique challenges to the inhabitants of the Old World. The New World challenged Old World ideas about humanity, slavery, politics, and especially religion. As Old World theologians tried to incorporate the New World in their theology, they turned to antique sources to explore the unity of humanity. Suddenly understanding pre-Christian peoples became much more important to Christian intellectuals and Christian missionaries alike. This was primarily because, like the indigenous New World peoples, people who lived before Christ had no knowledge of Christ. Augustine wrote with regard to antique accounts of peoples: "Either the written accounts of certain races are completely unfounded; or, if such races do exist, they are not human; or, if they are human, they are descended from Adam."[1]

Such races did clearly exist, the New World was living proof (as it were). In the encounter with the New World both question of the humanity of these peoples and their relationship to Adam became central. Whether the peoples of the New World were sons and daughters of Adam and Eve was an urgent question for sixteenth-century Europeans. The practice of and debate about Amerindian slavery dominated conversations in Old World courts and seminaries as well as New World missions. After a long century of debate and conflict the question of the humanity of Amerindians was resolved and an official church policy established, though the practice of Amerindian slavery lingered. The next challenge for Old World theologians was to explore the relationship between Adam and the Amerindians. In the search for the answer to the question "are these people descended from Adam" the comparative method in religion was born.

Beginning with the early missionaries to the New World, the act of comparing Amerindians and their practices with accounts from antiquity and the biblical narratives became a way to understand how the Amerindians could exist "without the knowledge of the true God." One of the most prominent New World missionaries and proponent of Amerindian rights, Bartolomé Las Casas, wrote:

> I say that not only have the Indians shown themselves to be very prudent peoples, with acute minds, having justly and prosperously governed their republics (so far as they could without faith and the knowledge of the true God), but they have equalled many diverse races of the past and present, much praised for government, way of life, and customs. And in following the rules of natural reason, they have even surpassed by not a little those who were the most prudent of all, such as the Greeks and Romans. This advantage ... will appear very clearly, if it please God, *when the Indian races are compared with others.*[2]

With this statement, the practice of comparing Amerindians with the Greeks and Romans was begun. During the sixteenth-century comparing Amerindians with Greek and Roman sources became a motif in many missionary accounts of the New World.

---

1. Augustine, *City of God* 16.8.
2. Las Casas, "Rationality," 115, emphasis added.

Introduction

Las Casas was not the only missionary to use the comparative method to demonstrate the "prudence" of the Amerindians and their ways of life. His contemporaries, Bernardino de Sahagún and José de Acosta, also compared Amerindians with Greeks and Romans.[3] A century after Las Casas, Sahagún, and Acosta, another missionary took up the practice of comparing Amerindians with texts from antiquity and introduced the possibility of "seeing" in the Amerindians the lives of the Greeks and Romans. His work is still cited as a pioneering text in comparative religion.[4] He was the Jesuit missionary Joseph François Lafitau.

Joseph Lafitau (1681–1746) was the author of *Moeurs des sauvages américains comparées aux moeurs des premiers temps* (1724). This book is an ambitious comparative work, examining the practices and beliefs of Amerindians in relation to Greek and Roman accounts. A central question for Lafitau was the very question Augustine posed: could he demonstrate that the Amerindians were the descendents of Adam? Lafitau traced the lineage of the ancients (Greeks and Romans) and the Amerindians to their shared point of origin in the Garden of Eden. He argued that, through the comparison of "customs"—cultural practices and beliefs—he could trace the living Amerindians back through time to their deceased ancestors, the ancients. From that conclusion, Lafitau then compared myths and stories with the Bible in order to show the roots of Christianity in those seemingly non-Christian peoples. From this comparison, Lafitau concluded the ancients and the Amerindians were in fact, descended from Adam.

In the history of the practice of comparison in the study of religion in particular, Lafitau's text has emerged as a pivotal document. His comparative work represents a moment in history where the world of the Enlightenment comes into stark relief. Lafitau's text gives his readers, from Edward Burnett Tylor to Michel de Certeau to David Chidester, a moment's pause as they reflect on the impact of the Enlightenment on the comparative study of religion.

---

3. After a survey of references to other worlds from Pliny to Saint Clement, José de Acosta assured his readers that the ancients knew of the New World. "From all this it may be safely assumed that there was some knowledge of the New World among the ancients, although there is almost nothing in the ancient authors' works that has particular reference to this America of ours and the West Indies as a whole." But even the lack of particular reference to "this America of ours" did not stop missionaries like Acosta from scanning ancient authors to find points of comparison with Amerindians. De Acosta, *Historia.*, 41.

4. Chidester, *Savage Systems*.

Work Useful to Religion and the Humanities

LAFITAU'S "USEFUL WORK": A SURVEY OF CITATIONS

In the preface to his comparative study of the Amerindians with that of "first times" Lafitau wrote he hoped his work would be "useful to religion and the humanities."[5] In some ways, Lafitau's hope was realized. This work began as a project to investigate the question of why the Jesuit missionary Joseph Lafitau was the "first ethnographer of the New World" to some scholars,[6] the "father of cultural anthropology" to other scholars,[7] an "acute Jesuit" to some,[8] and, finally, the founder of modern ethnography to yet others.[9] Lafitau's work, *Moeurs*, has been used by numerous scholars from Francis Parkman to Lewis Henry Morgan to Arthur C. Parker to Daniel Richter. His work is regularly cited by scholars interested in details about Amerindian life, especially Iroquois life, in the early colonial period of the North American Northeast.[10] However, regardless of their discipline, none of the scholars mentioned above, from Francis Parkman to David Chidester, are interested in Lafitau's comparative system or his understanding of religion. Instead, these authors mine Lafitau's text for details about Amerindian life, especially Iroquois life, and disregard his other goals.

There are an eclectic mix of scholars who consult Lafitau's work on religion and anthropology. Most significant for the study of religion, Lafitau is regularly mentioned by Edward Burnett Tylor. Tylor credits Lafitau with making the initial observation that Lewis Henry Morgan will later develop into a classificatory system for family structure among the Iroquois:[11] "Father Lafitau . . . carefully described among the Iroquois and Hurons the system of kinship to which [Lewis Henry] Morgan has since given the name of 'classificatory,' where the mother's sisters are reckoned as mothers, and so on."[12] Tylor is not the only scholar to credit Lafitau with insightful contributions to their particular field of study, be it anthropology, ethnology or

---

5. Lafitau, *Moeurs*, 269.
6. Sayre, *Les Sauvages Americains*, 138.
7. Bangert, *A History of the Society of Jesus*, 360.
8. Tylor, "American Aspects of Anthropology," 228.
9. Motsch, *Lafitau et L'émergence*.
10. Parkman, *France and England in North America*; Parkman, *The Jesuits in North America*; Parkman, *Pioneers of France*; Morgan, *Ancient Society*; Morgan, *League*; Parker, *Iroquois Uses of Maize*; Parker, *Parker on the Iroquois*; Richter, "War and Culture."
11. Lafitau, *Moeurs*, cxi.
12. Tylor, "American Aspects of Anthropology," 229.

Introduction

comparative religion. Lafitau's work is cited in many histories of anthropology and ethnology from the nineteenth and twentieth-centuries.

By way of introduction it is important to see the place Lafitau's text has had in the history of anthropology, even though there is much disagreement about the breadth and depth Lafitau's contribution. In 1934 Alfred C. Haddon wrote in *History of Anthropology* that Lafitau "regarded primitive peoples as living witnesses of stages in the history of humanity."[13] This reading of Lafitau's text was followed by Penniman in his history of anthropology. He wrote that Lafitau "interprets ancient peoples in light of modern savages."[14] Both Haddon and Penniman felt that Lafitau's text deserved some recognition in their history of anthropology, though neither summary is particularly complete. Frederick Teggart offers a similar one-line reference that Lafitau "noted parallels between customs of . . . indians [sic] and those of the early Greeks."[15] Sol Tax, in a history of anthropology entitled "From Lafitau to Radcliffe-Brown" mentions that Lafitau, when describing the matrilineal system of the Iroquois "hit . . . by chance on the classificatory system" that would dominate 19th century anthropological discussions of kinship.[16] These short assessments reflect the primary goals of Lafitau's work and acknowledge the contribution *Moeurs* made to the early history of anthropology, though they disregard his religious perspective and theological agenda.

Probably the best consideration of Lafitau's work prior to the critical edition of *Moeurs* by William Fenton and Elizabeth Moore in 1977 is Margaret Hodgen's appraisal in her 1964 book *Early Anthropology in the Sixteenth and Seventeenth Centuries*.[17] In this work, Hodgen gives Lafitau's work a careful review. She outlines the structure of Lafitau's larger argument about the relationship between Amerindians and what can be learned about antique and pre-Christian peoples: "Pére Lafitau insisted that the religion of the Indians was basically the same as that of the ancients, and cited innumerable rites and practices which seemed to bear a striking resemblance to those of the Greeks at the time of Homer and the Hebrews at

---

13. Haddon, *History of Anthropology*.
14. Penniman, *A Hundred Years of Anthropology*, 46.
15. Teggart, *The Idea of Progress*, 13.
16. Tax, "From Lafitau to Radcliffe-Brown," 445–46. While his title uses Lafitau's name, Tax's article says little more about Lafitau than the above quote.
17. Hodgen, *Early Anthropology*.

the time of Moses."[18] More than any other author, Hodgen represents the core of Lafitau's argument: "Not only did Pére Lafitau indicate innumerable parallels between American Indians and the Greeks and Romans, with reference to his chief interest, the institution of religion, but he showed the same meticulous interest in the collection of correspondences in government, marriage, family, education, the occupations of men and women, hunting and fishing, the disposition of the dead, and language."[19] Few other reviewers read Lafitau as thoroughly as Hodgen. In her attempt to trace the history of the early modern practice of anthropology, she credits Lafitau as the "most mature and competently stated argument" regarding the connections, real or imagined, between Amerindians and the peoples of antiquity.[20] She is the only scholar to recognize the import of Lafitau's contribution to the practice of comparison in the history of anthropology.

Most important for the purposes of this work, Hodgen also points to a similarity between Lafitau and Tylor. She states in her conclusion regarding Lafitau that "He attempted . . . *not unlike Tylor at a much later date*, to demonstrate that the customs of the American Indians displayed 'singular and curious traces; or 'vestiges' of the cultures and religions of the earliest historical peoples, namely, the Greeks at the time of Homer and the Hebrews at the time of Moses; that all men came from the same inaugural stem; but that the Indians, as savages, represented an earlier and older phase of human development and occupied a lower place than civil man in the temporalized chain of being."[21] This statement is provocative: Hodgen points out a demonstrable relationship between Lafitau's comparative system and Tylor's comparative system that has not been explored in any detail. This similarity, present in a deep reading of Lafitau's text, is the starting-place for this study.

Despite the recognition given Lafitau's work in the history of anthropology, histories of the Society of Jesus, remarkably, neglect him.[22] The Catholic Encyclopedia (1910) says "After Charlevoix, Lafitau was the most remarkable historian and naturalist ever sent to Canada by the Society of

---

18. Ibid., 314.
19. Ibid., 348.
20. Ibid.
21. Ibid., 446.

22. Lafitau receives no mention in these major histories of the Society of Jesus: Barthel, *The Jesuits*; Lacouture, *Jesuits*; Alden, *The Making of an Enterprise*.

Jesus."²³ The New Catholic Encyclopedia (1967) mentions *Moeurs*, Lafitau's second book *Histoire des découvertes et des conquetes des Portugais dans le Nouveau-Monde* (1733), and Lafitau's contribution to the eighteenth century Jesuit periodical *Mémoires de Trévoux*, but does not make any claims for Lafitau's intellectual contribution to the history of anthropology or comparative religion.²⁴ William V. Bangert mentions Lafitau only once in his *History of the Society of Jesus* (1972) as having been "recognized as the Father of Cultural Anthropology" but does not develop his assessment of Lafitau's contribution to either the order or the discipline of anthropology any further.²⁵

One outstanding exception to this lack of Jesuit interest in Lafitau is Carl F. Starkloff's (SJ) assessment in *Common Testimony: Ethnology and Theology in the Customs of Joseph Lafitau* (2001).²⁶ Starkloff attributes Lafitau's absence in many Society of Jesus histories to his lack of an overt theological agenda: "That lack of Jesuit interest in him today is an oversight that Lafitau himself would no doubt readily excuse, since his available literary works *say little that identifies him as a Jesuit*. Not that he sought to hide the fact; it is rather that his interests were not focused on in-house matters, but on the study of the cultures to which he had been missioned."²⁷ Not only was Lafitau interested in those other cultures, he was intrigued by Europe's past as well. Lafitau attempted to construct and justify a universal history of humanity. Starkloff analyzes *Moeurs* in order to give Lafitau the recognition he deserves and to provide an understanding of Lafitau's "systematic theology" as a major contribution to the Society of Jesus and the contemporary efforts of the order's mission. ²⁸

The 1977 publication of Fenton and Moore's edition of *Moeurs* marked the first translation of Lafitau's work into English. The Champlain Society

---

23. Lindsay, "Joseph Francois Lafitau."

24. Bannon, "Joseph Lafitau"; *Memoires Pour L'histoire Des Sciences & Des Beaux Arts*.

25. Bangert, *A History of the Society of Jesus*.

26. Starkloff, SJ, *Common Testimony*.

27. Ibid., 4, emphasis added. It is true the monogenesist approach that Lafitau argues is not exclusively Jesuit. Lafitau's text is still a theological text, driven by the desire to see Christianity at the origin of all religion beliefs and practices.

28. Ibid., 5. "Our 'heuristic' question here is, then, Which [sic] elements of Lafitau's theoretical system must remain as past history, and which can be retrieved in studying the interaction between faith and culture?" Starkloff wants to examine and reinstate the systematic theology he sees present in Lafitau's work, *Moeurs*, into Jesuit practice.

edition was translated by Elizabeth L. Moore with a critical introduction by William N. Fenton.[29] The introduction reflects Fenton's interest in Iroquois culture and the anthropology of Amerindian tribes.[30] In terms of Lafitau's biography, Fenton and Moore provide the most extensive exploration of Lafitau's life and works to date. Fenton appreciates Lafitau's contribution to the scholarly world and calls Lafitau the "eighteenth century's only true comparative ethnologist" because of his "systematic and original mind."[31]

Unlike many others interested in Lafitau's text, Fenton examines Lafitau's sources, such as José de Acosta. Fenton acknowledges the difficulty of tracing many of Lafitau's references, however. Fenton writes that *Moeurs* is "poorly annotated" and that Lafitau relied heavily on his memory of texts "sometimes without going to the originals himself."[32] Nonetheless, Fenton and Moore position Lafitau as a pivotal thinker in the fields of ethnology and anthropology that will "take off from him in the nineteenth-century."[33]

Lafitau has had a solid place in the French intellectual tradition since *Moeurs* was published. Voltaire's *The Philosophy of History* (1766) features a segment critically directed at *Moeurs*.[34] Claiming Lafitau made a rather simplistic argument, Voltaire then turned the point of his sharp wit on Lafitau's text: "Lafiteau [sic] at length makes the Americans descend from the ancient Greeks, for which opinion he assigns the following reasons. The Greeks had their fables, the Americans have also fables; the first Greeks went a-hunting, the Americans also hunt; the first Greeks had oracles, the Americans have their sorcerers; there were dances performed at the feasts of the Greeks, the Americans dance. It must be allowed that these are very convincing reasons."[35] Voltaire found Lafitau's comparative method laughable, mocking Lafitau's conclusions regarding how the inhabitants of the New World have been governed, the role of the natural world on

---

29. Lafitau, *Moeurs*.

30. See Fenton, *The False Faces*; Fenton, *The Great Law*; Fenton, *The Iroquois Eagle Dance*.

31. Lafitau, *Moeurs*, lxvii.

32. Ibid., xii.

33. Ibid., li.

34. Voltaire, *The Philosophy of History*, 35–41.

35. Ibid., 36.

Introduction

Amerindian customs, and what role New World inhabitants played in the history of humanity's conquests and territorial expansions.[36]

However, Voltaire's *The Philosophy of History* followed the structure and form of Lafitau's book, even though he disagreed with many, if not all, of Lafitau's conclusions. Voltaire discussed the origin of the soul, religion, humanity, forms of government, flora, fauna, and made connections with Egyptians, Jews and Greeks. Voltaire used the same authorities for his argument against Lafitau that Lafitau used in his text: Herodotus, Strabo, Xenophon and the Hebrew Bible.[37] Even though his writing was structurally similar to Lafitau's work and he was educated at a Jesuit college, Voltaire's anti-clericism kept him from seeing Lafitau's work in a serious light. Voltaire went so far as to have argued that China was superior to the west primarily because there was no sacerdotal rule in Chinese history.[38]

In the eighteenth-century intellectuals looked to antiquity in an attempt to understand the variety of religions in the New World. In *The Eighteenth-Century Confronts the Gods*, Frank Manuel argues that intellectuals blended Greco-Roman "paganism" and New World "paganism" together in order to interpret and understand both antique history and the New World. Thinkers such as Lafitau saw the peoples of the New World and the people from antiquity as parallel traditions. As Manuel explains: "The parallel always worked both ways: it infused meaning into savage rites in the new world, and at the same time it became the key to a reinterpretation

---

36. Ibid., 41. "A reflection might be made upon the nations of the new world, which father Lafitau has omitted, which is, that the people distant from the tropics have always been invincible; and that those people who were nearest the topics have almost always been subdued by monarchs. It was for a long time the same way on our continent; but we do not find that the people of Canada have ever attempted to subjugate Mexico, in the manner that the Tartars spread themselves over Asia and Europe. It should seem that the Canadians were never sufficiently numerous to detach colonies into other parts" (36-37).

37. Pomeau, *La Religion De Voltaire*. It is interesting to note that Voltaire attended Louis Le Grand College from 1704-1711. Lafitau was a teacher there for the first ten years of his formation, which ended in 1711. It is possible that he and Voltaire had met, perhaps even in class.

38. See Voltaire, *The Philosophy of History*, 39-40. See also Northeast, *The Parisian Jesuits*, 47-52. Northeast argues that Jesuits and Philosophes shared a common intellectual endeavor. "Jesuit commentators scarcely differed from Voltaire and the writers of the Enlightenment in their concept of imagination and their general critical assumptions." This similarity represents a point of contact between religious and secular "men of letters" rather than a source of conflict. Northeast's argument highlights the fruitful exchange that philosophes and Jesuits shared in the eighteenth century Enlightenment world.

of the spirit of the ancients."³⁹ This seems particularly true of Lafitau's understanding of both the New World and antiquity; in fact, Manuel points to Lafitau as one of the primary sources for this particular viewpoint.

Despite this observation about the relationship between antiquity and the eighteenth century intellectual world, and Voltaire's pointed review, few contemporary scholars are interested in Lafitau's relationship to the Enlightenment. An exception is Michele de Certeau. De Certeau argues that Lafitau was an important transitional thinker on the cusp of the Enlightenment, demonstrating the shift from a worldview dominated by religion to a worldview dominated by science.⁴⁰ De Certeau based his argument on the frontspiece of *Moeurs*. He argued Lafitau was part of the intellectual transition from religion to science and that Lafitau's work indicated the beginning of the shift from a biblically based vision of human development to an anthropologically based one.⁴¹ De Certeau alluded to Lafitau's "ambiguous" personal position, asserting that Lafitau embodied the scientific enterprise yet came from a theological vantage point. Lafitau's scientific enterprise was one that began with theological presuppositions; however, de Certeau insisted, Lafitau betrayed those very presuppositions in a "displacement of theology toward anthropology."⁴² As a consequence of that 'displacement' rather than a straightforward replacement of anthropology for theology, Lafitau's work was relegated to historical anonymity.⁴³ Lafitau's anthropological writing was "embarrassing" to his contemporaries and to later scholars because of his theological tendencies, and so, according to de Certeau, Lafitau's work was "disowned by the intelligentsia that he hoped at once to serve and to conquer."⁴⁴

De Certeau did not offer any suggestions about exactly what it means to say that Lafitau was a "transitional intellectual" nor why anthropologists and other scholars have called upon Lafitau and his writing when claiming historical authority for their anthropological arguments. De Certeau's argument was based on the interpretation of images in the frontspiece rather

---

39. Manuel, *The Eighteenth Century*, 19. For other references to Lafitau, see 146, 156, 192, 198.

40. De Certeau, "Writing vs. Time," 37–64.

41. Ibid.

42. Ibid., 57.

43. Ibid., 37–64. Lafitau's text seems well recognized in the history of anthropology; see above.

44. Ibid.

Introduction

than Lafitau's text itself. Also, he contended that the form of Lafitau's book was "theological" and the content was "scientific" but did not offer examples of how the form was "theological." Regardless, de Certeau maintained that Lafitau was a modern in pre-modern intellectual attire.

De Certeau's article is influential and inspired two very different and profound responses. Anthony Pagden's 1992 response to de Certeau's argument that Lafitau is a "modern" is an emphatic "no."[45] Pagden is not interested in Lafitau's theology, his religious perspective, nor his comparative system. Instead, Pagden argues that Lafitau was concerned with social forces that shape human behavior, such as political organization and family structure. Because he was concerned with social issues, Pagden sees Lafitau as qualitatively different than either Sahagún or Acosta both of whom utilize a method similar to Lafitau's.

Pagden acknowledges Lafitau's commitment to precision and detail in his description of indigenous cultures. "His descriptions of Indian society seem to us to be far closer to the truths of the Indian world . . . only because his terms of reference are closer to our own than any available to equally perceptive, equally 'honest' men of a century earlier."[46] Lafitau is capable of appearing modern because he represents Amerindian culture in ways modern people can relate to but Pagden explicitly challenges de Certeau's claim that Lafitau is "modern:"[47] "[I]f we step back from Lafitau's concern for precise ethnographical description, his modernism dissolves. For his perceptions are harnessed to an enterprise which is wholly alien to the modern mind: the attempt to demonstrate the truth of the Christian religion by the degree to which races which had had no knowledge of the Gospel unknowingly imitated the rituals and believe, the 'Symbolic Theology,' of both Jew and Gentile."[48] Pagden argues that Lafitau was motivated by a social concern, a desire to understand what humans do. (His desire to describe and compare burial rites is one example.) But Pagden ultimately argues that Lafitau's work was an act of Christian apologetics, designed only to show the truth of Christianity. From Pagden's perspective, Lafitau did not provide a window on Amerindian life because he did not see indigenous cultures on their own terms. He argues that Lafitau did not reflect a modernist outlook but rather a pre-modern, Christian,

---

45. Pagden, *The Fall of Natural Man*, 4.
46. Ibid.
47. Ibid.
48. Ibid.

and ultimately Eurocentric perspective. "For Lafitau . . . the savage has an identity only in so far as he has a meaning, and he has meaning only in so far as he has a determinate and measurable relationship to 'us.'"⁴⁹ Pagden concludes that Lafitau's text is by Europeans, for Europeans, and, in the end, only about Europeans.

In his 2001 work *Lafitau et l'émergence du discours ethnographique*, Andreas Motsch picks up de Certeau's question about Lafitau's modernism. Motsch answers de Certeau with an equally emphatic "yes." He argues that Lafitau was the first modern ethnographer.⁵⁰ He builds on de Certeau's argument that Lafitau was a transitional intellectual, bridging the gap between a modern, scientific worldview and a pre-modern religious worldview. Motsch's intent is to demonstrate that Lafitau was the transitional intellectual of the pre-Enlightenment era that de Certeau had suggested. Motsch believes that Lafitau brought the Catholic church into the modern world by introducing a way of viewing Amerindians that led, eventually, to rationalism and secularization.⁵¹ In order to accomplish the goal of modernizing the Catholic church, Motsch argues that Lafitau abandoned the medieval, religious worldview of the Roman Catholic church and embraced his own rationalist approach. Lafitau's rationalist approach, he argues, contributed to the secularist method that eventually comes to dominate all further discourse about the relationship between Europeans and Amerindians: "L'auteur des Moeurs reconnaîtra deux choses: d'abord, que la vision théocentrique du monde et l'image chrétienne de l'homme dont l'Église a hérité de la scolastique du Moyen Âge perdent leur validité devant l'hétérogénéité de l'Amérique et de ses habitants ; ensuite, que l'altérité américaine non seulement remet radicalement en question l'autorité interprétative de l'Église, mais semble en outre donner raison aux ennemis de l'Église, en confirmant les nouveaux paradigmes rationalistes."⁵² Motsch argues Lafitau

---

49. Pagden, *European Encounters*, 148. Pagden's primary objection to understanding Lafitau as a "modern" is that Lafitau's approach is "wholly alien" to the "modern mind." (ibid., 4) This opens the question of what constitutes a "modern mind," particularly with regard to the study of "pre-modern" peoples. Since it is my argument that Lafitau and Tylor both use Amerindians to "see" the past, there are two responses to Pagden's thesis. First, neither Lafitau and Tylor are "modern" by Pagden's standards or second that Lafitau is not as "wholly alien" as Pagden concludes because Tylor uses the same type of system for comparing cultures.

50. Motsch, *Lafitau Et L'émergence*. This book is not available in English. All translations are my own.

51. Ibid.

52. Ibid., 18. The author of *Moeurs* [Lafitau] will recognize two things: initially, that

Introduction

adopted his rationalist system through the intellectual exercise of comparing Amerindian with pre-Christian Europeans, claiming Lafitau's method of comparison in *Moeurs* demonstrated that if the Amerindians and the ancients shared the same customs, they must, by the same token, have shared the same origin.[53]

Motsch argues Lafitau's practice of ethnography was grounded in his understanding of the idea of time and history. Motsch believes that Lafitau rejected the European assumption that the lack of writing technologies equals a lack of history. He argues that Lafitau left this understanding behind and moved to comparative ethnography in order to account for the diversity of peoples and practices that he found during his tenure in the New World. Lafitau's comparison of Amerindian customs with the customs described in antique texts gave the Amerindians a history because of the similarity of their customs with those of the ancient Greeks, Romans, Hebrews, etc. Lafitau understood that history is separate from the technology of writing, which was why he developed this particular ethnography: "L'ethnographe comprend la différence de l'écriture amérindienne comme une « absence de lettres alphabétiques ». Ce constat renvoie à la fois à l'absence de technique alphabétique et au fait que cette absence influence et oriente la façon dont se constitue la tradition de l'histoire, si ce n'est la mémoire elle-même."[54] In other words, the absence of writing does not equal the absence of history. Even though Amerindians and the ancients were separated by time, their history was not lost or missing. Their history was "found" in antique texts—it was already written. Lafitau was however

---

the theocentric vision of the world and the Christian image of man which the Church inherited from the scholastic Middle Ages lose their validity before the heterogeneity of America and its inhabitants; then, that the American otherness not only radically calls in question the interpretative authority of the Church, but seems moreover to give reason to the enemies of the Church, by confirming the new rationalist paradigms.

53. Ibid., 15. The ethnographer understands the difference of the Amerindian "C'est par le biais d'une comparaison des moeurs que Lafitau va désormais entreprendre la quête des origines des Amérindiens et des peuples occidentaux. Il conclut que si ces sociétés partagent les mêmes coutumes, elles doivent aussi partager la même origine." It is by the means of a comparison of manners that Lafitau from now on will undertake the search of the origins of Amérindians and the Western people. He concludes that if these societies share the same habits, they must also share the same origin.

54. Ibid., 270. The ethnographer understands the difference of the Amerindian writing as an "absence of alphabetical letters." This report returns at the same time to the absence of alphabetical technique and the fact that this absence influences and directs the way in which the tradition of the history is constituted, if it is not the memory itself.

concerned to show how Amerindians remembered their history and to fill in what parts they did not remember from antique texts.

Motsch argues the answer to this dilemma of written history versus actual history leads to an anthropology that secured for the church a rationalist argument about the existence of Amerindians by giving them a history, antique history, even though they lacked the traditional means of demonstrating that history, i.e. writing. The disunity of diverse geographies (the separation of the New World from the Old World) is overcome by a unity of customs and that established the universality and supremacy of Christianity: "Pour cet homme d'Église, deux vérités s'affrontent sans qu'une solution pointe à l'horizon. D'un côté, on affirme que tout être sur la terre est une créature de Dieu et mérite à ce titre d'être reconnue et respectée. De l'autre, on constate, dans le passé comme dans le présent, une diversité de l'expérience humaine qui semble contredire l'unité déclarée de la création."[55] Motsch centers his understanding of Lafitau's significance on the way that Lafitau used time (i.e. his understanding of history) and space (i.e. material conditions) in *Moeurs*.

> [L]e temps est conçu comme une entité objective qui existe en soi, en dehors des phénomènes, et comme un flux linéaire d'organisation et de mesure encadrant l'existence humaine. L'espace est vu comme un espace physique, fini et inanimé, et sa conceptualisation se fonde sur l'espace naturel qui fournit à l'être humain les conditions matérielles de son existence. l'adoption de la distinction empirique entre la dimension matérielle et la dimension spirituelle et symbolique des choses, entre la nature objective et les perceptions subjectives, est concomitante de la scission du discours ethnographique en une approche scientifique et une approche culturelle et cosmologique."[56]

---

55. Ibid., 17. For this man of the church, two truths clash without a solution appearing on the horizon. On a side, one [truth] affirms that all to be on the ground [earth] is a creature of God and for this reason deserves to be recognized and respected. [On the] Other, one notes, in the past as in the present, a diversity of the human experience which seems to contradict the declared unity of creation.

56. Ibid., 266. In the spirit of Lafitau, time is conceived as an objective entity which exists in oneself, apart from the phenomena, and like a linear flow of organization and measurement framing the human existence. Space is seen as a physical, finished and inanimate space, and its conceptualization is based on the natural space which provides human beings the material conditions of their existence. The adoption of the empirical distinction between material dimension and spiritual dimension and symbolic system of the things, between objective nature and subjective perceptions, is concomitant ethnographic split of the discourse in a scientific approach and a cultural and cosmological approach.

Introduction

Lafitau, in effect, provided Amerindians with a history so that they could be incorporated into Christendom. Motsch argues this comparative history, which negated Amerindian's physical space (the New World) but provided them with a history (antiquity), then answered many of the nagging questions about how the Amerindians could have existed for so long without European knowledge of them or biblical references to their existence. Lafitau's intellectual system brought Amerindians under the wing of the church and removed the theological challenge posed by of the existence of the New World. It was not important where or when Amerindians were to be found, it is only important that they were part of the unified world of Christianity.

Motsch argues that Lafitau folded Amerindians into the unity of God's creation through the comparison of Amerindian practices, rituals and lives to ancient practices, rituals and lives. As a result of this inclusion, Amerindians are "de-ontologized:" "L'espace amérindien est en fin de compte désontologise, c'est-à-dire désanimé et déritualisé ; il est objectivé en simple espace physique et, enfin, naturalisé et fonctionnalisé à un point tel qu'il coïncide avec l'espace empirique et utilitaire de l'ethnographe. L'acceptation d'une certaine relativité culturelle dans l'organisation et la gestion de l'espace empirique se trouve, à la fin du parcours descriptif et analytique, enfermée dans la logique de l'ethnographe."[57] Motsch argues that for Lafitau, New World lands are unimportant for understanding the history and existence of Amerindians. Through the use of ancient texts to provide Amerindians with a history, the space of the New World is no longer a space in its own right but merely a location where the material conditions of Amerindian life have been met.

Motsch argues Lafitau's ethnocentrism was an inevitably result of his social and historical context. But for Motsch, what is really important is that Lafitau made the critically important first comparative step, showing that Amerindian customs are the same as European customs, and their history is the same as European history. The Amerindians are the ancient Europeans. As a result of Lafitau's argument, Motsch concludes the existence of Amerindians in their New World location did not call into question the

---

57. Ibid. Amerindian space is in the final analysis de-ontologized, i.e. de-animated and de-ritualized; it is objectified in simple physical space and, finally, naturalized and functionalized at a point such as it coincides with the empirical space and utilized by the ethnographer. The acceptance of a certain cultural relativity in the organization and the management of empirical space is, at the end of the descriptive and analytical course, locked up in the logic of the ethnographer.

ultimate position of the church and the universality of Christianity. Here Motsch sees the first step in Enlightenment thinking. Lafitau was using categories that were not strictly theological, though they may have been theologically informed. The use of these rationalist categories moved the church beyond the more dogmatic approach that confronted Devil-worshipping savages with God-fearing Europeans to seeing New World peoples as antique peoples and thereby advanced the church's modernist perspective. While Lafitau's point of view still ultimately preserved the supremacy of Europe, Motsch argues he opened up the possibility for understanding native peoples without an *apriori* shroud of judgment. Lafitau accomplished this by inserting Amerindians into European history and thus made them worthy of further study in their own right.

Motsch concludes that this comparative method is what makes Lafitau the founder of modern ethnology. He concludes: "Bien que le discours des moeurs ne soit pas entièrement rationnel en raison des présupposés théologiques de l'auteur, il offre néanmoins une description rationnelle de l'altérité amérindienne et fait à juste titre de Lafitau le fondateur de l'ethnographie moderne."[58] Lafitau's unique work and particular intellectual position as an proto-Enlightenment thinker make him the ideal person to have repositioned the church in response to her rationalist critics.

Motsch's reading of Lafitau's text is significant and ground-breaking but it only goes so far. He brings out Lafitau's novelty and emphasizes the importance of Lafitau's text for the creation of an ethnological subject. However, because Motsch makes no attempt to see Lafitau's text in relation to other New World missionary ethnographers, his understanding of Lafitau is somewhat ahistorical. Lafitau's work is not completely anomalous in the history of New World contact documents. Bartolomé Las Casas, Bernardino de Sahagún, and José de Acosta utilized similar methods and, while they may have been more invested in the missionary process, they nonetheless ask comparative questions similar to Lafitau's. In Motsch's final chapter he mentions Las Casas, Sahagún and Acosta in passing but does not see them contributing to or showing signs of what Lafitau attempted to accomplish in *Moeurs*: "Si ma contextualisation passe dans les deux cas [de la nouveauté de l'Amérique, une nouveauté qui recouvre des significations quelque peu différentes entre le XVI et le XVIII siècle] par le registre historique,

58. Ibid., 271. Although the discourse of Moeurs is not entirely rational because of the theological presuppositions of the author, it offers nevertheless a rational description of the Amerindian otherness and rightly makes Lafitau the founder of the modern ethnography.

Introduction

ce n'est pas parce que j'attribue à l'histoire un pouvoir d'agencement, mais simplement à cause de la valeur heuristique de l'exercice."[59] The one and a half centuries of contact literature and work on the part of other missionary ethnographers contributed to Lafitau's text as much, if not more, than the forces Motsch identifies—the Reformation, counter-Reformation and anticlerical impulses in France. While these may certainly be factors, Lafitau is much more indebted to the course began by Las Casas, Sahagún and Acosta than Motsch acknowledges at the end of this book.[60]

While I agree with Motsch that Lafitau's text provided a Christian history for New World peoples, I do not agree that Lafitau thought antique history replaced or stood in for Amerindian history. I will argue instead that Lafitau sees antique history lived through his comparison of antiquity and the lives of the Amerindians, making adjustments to customs and practices to account for drift of time and difference of geographical location. Mostch argues Amerindians lost their identity—their ontology—in Lafitau's text. I argue that Lafitau understood Amerindians as the descendents of the ancients and thought therefore they shared a history with the ancients, but that he also understood Amerindians to have their own customs and adaptations and therefore had something to teach Europeans about the ancients.

This literature review has highlighted the major issues of understanding Lafitau's contribution to the scholarly world. This brief survey also demonstrates that Lafitau's hope that his work would be "useful to religion and the humanities" was at least partially realized. However, there is still more that can be learned from Lafitau's text. None of these secondary interpretations take two evident facts into account: first, that Lafitau's text had pre-Enlightenment comparative and theological predecessors in missionary writings from the very first moment of contact. Bartolomé Las Casas, Bernardino de Sahagún and José de Acosta all wrote early comparative texts about indigenous religion and Christianity. Secondly many nineteenth and twentieth-century interpretations neglect Lafitau as a Roman Catholic missionary whose interest in missionizing, while secondary to his other intellectual goals, was still his primary method of interacting with the

---

59. Ibid., 18. If my contextualization passes in both cases of the innovation (novelty) of America, a novelty which covers with the somewhat different significances between the XVI and the XVIII century by the historical register, it is not because I attribute to history a fitting organizing power or influence capacity, but simply because of the heuristic value of the exercise. The two cases are the innovation/novelty of American and second, the differences between the 16th and 18th centuries.

60. See ibid., 271–73.

indigenous peoples of what is now northeast Canada. What I am adding to these understandings is a vision of how Lafitau's comparative method can be appreciated in relation to theological and comparative positions of the other comparativists that precede him—namely Las Casas, Sahagún, and Acosta—and one who follows him: Tylor.

Scholars' difficulty understanding Lafitau is linked to the underlying problem of the relationship between religion and the Enlightenment. It is important to remember the central role played by Enlightenment thought in order properly to appreciate Lafitau's place in comparative religion. The role of religion in the Enlightenment has recently been revisited and re-interrogated.[61] Peter Gay argues that the Enlightenment philosophes were attempting a dialectic that balanced the antique (Roman) past of Cicero, Seneca and company with a rapidly expanding modern time. He argues that the philosophes wanted to find an answer to the question of how to put the ancients into dialog with the modern world.[62]

Following Gay's important study, the Enlightenment has been understood as a unified intellectual endeavor to understand ancient and modern paganism. This unified understanding of the Enlightenment as anti-religious, as a movement toward secularization, has been recently called into question. Dorinda Outram argues that there is little scholarly agreement about the "chronological, geographical and social confines of the Enlightenment, let alone any real interest in defining Enlightenment in terms of a coherent programme."[63] She traces the Enlightenment's borders and concludes that it is far more common to "see a continuity throughout the whole eighteenth century" rather than a sharp break that indicates the arrival of the Enlightenment.[64] If we see the eighteenth-century in terms of continuity rather than abrupt change, Lafitau finds his place among the many intellectuals interested in the comparative study of religion.[65] Though as scholars such as Gay and Pagden refuse to consider Lafitau as part of the Enlightenment world because he *was* religious, he struggled with this

61. Sheehan, "Enlightenment."
62. Gay, *The Enlightenment*, 8.
63. Outram, *The Enlightenment*, 8.
64. Ibid.
65. Ibid., 40. "Increasing interest in other religions, was also to lead to the study of religion as a human creation, rather than a revelation by the Divine of itself. This new focus is revealed, for example, in David Hume's 1757 *Natural History of Religion*, and in growing interest throughout the century in what we would now call the field of 'comparative religion.'"

same dialogic understanding of the New World and the antique world as the *philosophes*.

If, following the lead of scholars such as Outram and Darrin McMahon, we do not assume that "religion" and "Enlightenment" are incompatible, Lafitau's text contributes to the conversation about religion and the religions that began in the sixteenth century.[66] Instead of struggling to include the seemingly pre-modern Lafitau in the modern world of the Enlightenment, Lafitau's text becomes one dot on the line of efforts to compare religious phenomena over time, pre- and post- Enlightenment, demonstrating intellectual continuity where there was once thought to be a sharp break.

In this study, therefore, I will trace the roots of that comparative approach through Lafitau's pre-Enlightenment predecessors, the first missionary-ethnographers in the New World, Bartolomé Las Casas, Bernardino de Sahagún, and José de Acosta. I argue that, in light of the scholarly acknowledgement of Lafitau's intellectual contribution, the comparative method for the cross-cultural study of religion has its roots in the earliest missionary contact in the New World rather than in the nineteenth-century. I will trace the lineage of the comparative method through those Catholic missionaries to the recognized originator of that method, Edward Burnett Tylor. I do this in order to amend the current thinking of anthropology and comparative religion that has seen a sharp distinction between missionaries and anthropologists.

George Stocking is undoubted the leading expert on the history of anthropology.[67] However, in his understanding of the history of anthropology and particularly his understanding of Tylor's comparative method, he leaves out the pre-Enlightenment missionary-ethnographers, such as Las Casas, Sahagún, Acosta, and Lafitau. Tylor's comparative method is remarkably similar to these missionary-ethnographers as I will argue. Stocking, however, does not see the connection between Tylor and these missionary-ethnographers.

This is in part because of Stocking's understanding of the role of the Enlightenment in Tylor's thought. Stocking acknowledges Tylor's debt to the Enlightenment, particularly the work of David Hume. However, Stocking recognizes that Tylor was still tied to the Enlightenment worldview

---

66. McMahon, *Enemies of the Enlightenment*.

67. See Stocking, *Race, Culture, and Evolution*; Stocking, *Malinowski, Rivers, Benedict*; Stocking, *Victorian Anthropology*; Stocking, *After Tylor*.

and suggests that Tylor was in some ways almost a "survival" of the Enlightenment: "In some respects, he seems better viewed as a survival of the Enlightenment, a latter-day *philosophe* attacking theology, superstition, and 'all the practices of civilized life for which common sense can find no justification.' But if one follows the details of Tylor's intellectual development, both his links to the contemporary anthropological milieu and the impact of the Darwinian revolution are clear enough."[68] Tylor's intellectual development was deeply indebted to Darwinism, whatever relationship he may have maintained with the Enlightenment. And, as I will show, Tylor was devoted to eradicating "superstition" from religion as much as possible. However, Tylor was not anti-religion, per se; he understood Natural Religion to be the origin of religion as well as its highest attainment—the alpha and omega of religious evolution.

Stocking sees the Enlightenment as anti-religious and understands the root of the Enlightenment to be attacking religion. In other words, according to Stocking, Tylor's approach to religion is ultimately anti-religious just as the Enlightenment is anti-religious. But, as I argue, Tylor is not as anti-religious as Stocking believes. The historical path I will trace from Bartolomé Las Casas to Edward Burnett Tylor suggests that the Enlightenment does not mark an abrupt change in the understanding of comparative religion as Stocking argues. Instead, my work demonstrates the continuity of the comparative method from the discovery of the New World through the nineteenth-century and points to the fragmented nature of the Enlightenment once religion is incorporated into our understanding of it.

In order to support this argument, I begin chapter two with a discussion of the comparative works of Bartolomé Las Casas, Bernardino de Sahagún and José de Acosta. All three of these missionaries engaged in comparison by using Greek, Roman and biblical sources to show a similarity in practice or belief between the Amerindians and those authoritative European sources. In some sense, these missionaries were also (Christian) ethnographers, because their missionary aims required that they "understand" the culture they were trying to Christianize.

In chapter three, I explain Lafitau's comparative system. By comparing ancient and Amerindian peoples, Lafitau was able to illuminate

68. Stocking, *Victorian Anthropology*, 156 (footnote to Burrow, *Evolution and Society*). I think Stocking's use of the term "survival" is particularly important (and probably deliberate). Since Tylor was interested in seeing how "survivals" tell us what lingers from previous stages of development, it is appropriate that Tylor's thought be a "survival" of the Enlightenment.

ancient practices that Europeans had difficulty understanding and make an argument for a single, Christian, origin for religion. Lafitau's method was designed to show the genealogical connections between the ancients and the Amerindians. After demonstrating how Lafitau's "system" worked, I argue that his system allowed Lafitau to "see" ancient practices in living Amerindian cultures.

In chapter four, I compare Lafitau's system with Tylor's comparative anthropology. The similarity between Tylor's and Lafitau's models is explained by their mutual interest in using Amerindians to see previous stages of human life. Both Lafitau and Tylor argue that their method of comparison allowed them (and their readers) to see human history in living color. In contrast to Lafitau, however, Tylor argued missionaries planted the similarities they saw between cultures in those cultures. He felt that survivals demonstrated the connections between different stages of religious evolution and demonstrated those connections 'organically' as opposed to the unity that he argued that Catholic missionaries had read into their comparisons.

Although scholars have made a sharp distinction between thinkers such as Tylor and Lafitau, that sharp distinction is not supported by their texts. Lafitau and Tylor share significant understandings of religion in European history that challenge understandings of Lafitau as pre-modern and Tylor as modern. The similarities and differences in their approach to comparison demonstrates a change of emphasis on the role of religion in order to understand Europeans and indigenous peoples, but not a sharp break in either comparative method or explanation. The historical trajectory I will outline from Bartolomé Las Casas to Edward Burnett Tylor demonstrates the continuity of the comparative method in religion from the discovery of the New World through the nineteenth century.

2

The Comparative Method and Sacrifice in the New World

They are our fellow creatures, whom we are obliged to love as ourselves...

BERNARDINO DE SAHAGÚN
Historia general de las cosas de Nueva España

THE CHRISTIAN INJUNCTION FOR all Christians to love each other was a directive missionaries took very seriously. While we may, through the distance of history, reject some of their methods and manners for demonstrating Christian love, there is no doubt the missionaries who came to the New World took their vocation seriously. Part of their duty as missionaries was to embrace the Amerindians as brothers and sisters, descendents of Adam and Eve, members of the family of God in the church. While Europeans had not experienced the discovery of a land like the New World, they did have some ideas about peoples who had no knowledge of Christ or of Christianity. Many esteemed Greeks and Romans had lived and died before the revelation of Christ and therefore, had no knowledge of Christianity. The Renaissance world revered the "ancients" as they called Greek and Roman authors. They found many good and helpful ideas for Christian theology in those authors. For some of the missionaries to the New World, the Greeks and Romans established the model for how to understand non-Christian peoples who were created and loved by the Christian God. And so, as it applied to those pre-Christian peoples, the call to Christian love was also applied to those people who had been "discovered" in the New World.

In many ways, the early modern missionaries were closer to the antique authors they revered than they were to the Amerindians. The early modern missionaries understood their shared heritage with pre-Christian peoples. It was an important part of a missionary's intellectual development to explore the legacy of the Greeks and Romans as well as the church fathers. They learned philosophy and mathematics and all the cultural history that they could glean from the antique authors they studied at centers such as the University of Salamanca in Spain. Combined with this serious classical education, the missionaries brought their devotion to worldwide Christianity to the New World. And as the world expanded, so did their vision of their God-given task. As missionaries, these men endeavored to convert their Amerindian brethren. As ethnographers, they did everything they could to understand their new brothers and sisters as they understood their pre-Christian forefathers. This act of comparison, bringing Amerindians into the world of the antique authors, made them missionary-*ethnographers* more than just missionaries. Loving native peoples as themselves (and as they loved the pre-Christian ancients from their past) was the primary goal of missionary-ethnographers.

The thinkers under consideration in this chapter—Bartolomé Las Casas, Bernardino Sahagún, José de Acosta—were connected culturally and intellectually through their religious vocation in the New World. All were missionary-ethnographers and all had the best education their world had to offer. Sahagún was a member of the Franciscan order, Las Casas was a Dominican, and Acosta was a Jesuit. Most scholarly studies about missionaries focus on the members of a single order rather than seeing the orders in relationship to each other. However, cross-order comparison holds great promise for understanding how Europeans saw the New World and their relationship to it, as well as understanding the relationships and encounters between Europeans and Amerindians as well.[1]

---

1. See O'Malley, "Religious Orders of Men." While it is outside the parameters of my study to do more than suggest that there is a great promise for new insights that could be gathered in such a comparative enterprise, this chapter will compare these representatives of their respective orders with an acknowledgement of possibilities that will go unexplored.

Work Useful to Religion and the Humanities

The New World provided many challenges for religious orders, and the orders rose to the occasion, adapting to it in a variety of ways. As the well-trained and highly-educated religious they were, the particular missionary-ethnographers I will discuss in this chapter used their understandings of contemporary theological texts and debates in dialog with classical material to catalog, categorize, and catechize the inhabitants of the New World. These three missionary-ethnographers created a colonial discourse through their comparative efforts, "reshaping the structures of human knowledge" by incorporating New Spain and its inhabitants into Old World texts and identities.[2] Each missionary-ethnographer had his particular method for using antique texts to understand the New World. Bartolomé Las Casas used comparison between the New World and antiquity as a means of understanding the Amerindians. Bernardino de Sahagún wanted to understand Amerindian culture so he and future missionaries could better convert the Amerindians. José de Acosta examined Amerindian culture and compared it with antiquity in order to advise Europeans on issues of governance. All three missionary-ethnographers engaged in comparison in order to contextualize, shape and understand their particular moment the in encounter between Europeans and Amerindians.

In this chapter I will argue Las Casas, Sahagún, and Acosta constructed their comparisons of European and Amerindian cultures in order to Europeanize the Amerindians and to bring the Amerindians into the European world. Methodologically, all three missionaries appealed to the same authorities for their comparisons and set up their comparisons along similar lines. Using Aristotelian categories to establish the degree of civilization and basic rationality of the Amerindians in relation to European standards, these missionaries then turned to antique texts and biblical stories to find points of similarity with Amerindians. Once these points of similarity were established, the missionaries then drew theological conclusions about particular Amerindian beliefs and practices. As a result, their comparisons, while structurally similar, have slightly different goals and give some particular issues more prominence than others. All three used Aristotle to explain the relationship between the human and natural world in the New World. All three dealt with the issue of human sacrifice. Las Casas and Acosta rank indigenous civilization on a scale that emphasized

---

2. Ania Loomba, *Colonialism-Postcolonialism*, 57. Colonial discourse "reshaped existing structures of human knowledge . . . simultaneously a misrepresentation of reality and its reordering."

The Comparative Method and Sacrifice in the New World

the rationality of Amerindian civilization. Sahagún and Acosta discuss the role of the Devil in New World religion in order to explain practices they find unpalatable. Ultimately, all three looked to Greek and Roman sources to understand and explain the practices and beliefs they saw in the Amerindian communities where they spent their lives.

BARTOLOMÉ LAS CASAS (1484-1566)

Bartolomé Las Casas was one of the first Spaniards in the New World. Las Casas met some of the well-known conquistadors and accompanied Diego Velásquez on the conquest of Cuba in 1511. In 1514 Las Casas preached his now famous sermon condemning the Spanish for the way they treated natives peoples of the Americas. That sermon and his famous work *Brevísma relación de la destrucción de las Indias* have kept Las Casas on the forefront of any understanding of the early moments of European contact with the New World.[3] Las Casas's texts give a distinct picture of that time.

Las Casas is primarily known for his work *Brevísma relación de la destrucción de las Indias*. In this work, he described the atrocities perpetrated by the Spanish in the New World for European readers in the Old World.[4] This text was then used, by Las Casas himself as well as his contemporaries, to argue political and philosophical points regarding the treatment of Amerindians. Las Casas engaged in high profile political discourse about the enslavement of Amerindians and the illegitimacy of the European exploitation of the Amerindians. However, this work was not Las Casas's only statement against the slavery of Amerindians. In 1550 Las Casas engaged in a theological dispute with Juan Ginés de Sepúlveda at the court of Charles V.[5] That debate is certainly one of the most famous

---

3. *Brevísma* has been in print since it first appeared in 1566. It appeared first in English in 1583 and in Dutch 1578. It was translated and published in Latin in 1598 and in German in 1599. *Brevísma* spread the world of Spanish cruelty throughout Europe with astonishing speed. See David M. Traboulay, *Columbus and Las Casas* 187.

4. Bartolome Las Casas, *Devastation*.

5. This debate occupies a place of supreme importance for our understanding of the dynamics of Old World and New World contact. Lewis Hanke, *Aristotle*. "All this occurred in 1550, after Cortez had conquered Mexico, Pizarro had shattered the Inca empire, and many other lesser-known captains had carried the Spanish banners to far corners of the New World" (13). The debate did not attract enough attention sufficiently early in the conquest to actually make a significant difference to the fate of the Amerindians. "Of all the ideas churned up during the early tumultuous years of American history, none had a more dramatic application than the attempts made to apply to the natives

moments in the history of Christianity in the New World. Las Casas did not hesitate to condemn Europeans for their "barbarian" behaviors in the New World. It is important to bear in mind that Las Casas did not call for an end to the conquest, only an end to Amerindian slavery. Recognizing Amerindian independence and freedom from slavery was significant for Las Casas but he saw Christianization as the work of the conquest and the most important consequence of the European presence in the New World.

Brevísma relación de la destruccíón de las Indias was primarily a political text. Las Casas argued for the just governance of Amerindians by Europeans. It is also a theological text, but one in which Las Casas's theology served the larger political goals of European/Amerindians relations rather than the larger religio-cultural goals such as conversion, colonization, cultural exchange. For Las Casas, the question of rational capacities of the indigenous peoples of the New World was at the center of the debate with regard to the enslavement of Amerindians and the theological reading of Aristotle's concept of natural slavery.[6] These elements of Las Casas's texts made his work very high-profile both then and now; he is probably the most well-known of the missionary-ethnographers.[7]

Edmundo O'Gorman understands Las Casas's texts contributing to and strongly supporting the seventeenth-century idea that the "discovery" of America implied the coming of the new millennium.[8] O'Gorman is con-

---

there the Aristotelian doctrine of natural slavery: that one part of mankind is set aside by nature to be slaves in the service of masters born for a life of virtue free of manual labor . . . The controversy became so heated and the king's conscience so troubled over the question of how to carry on the conquest of the Indies in a Christian way that Charles V actually suspended all expeditions to America while a junta of foremost theologians, jurists and officials in the royal capital of Valladolid listened to the arguments of Las Casas and Sepúlveda" (13). See also Clyde Kluckhohn, *Anthropology*.

6. For a summary of the debate between Las Casas and Juan Ginés de Sepúlveda at the court of Charles V in 1550. See Lewis Hanke, *Aristotle*.

7. See Bartolome Las Casas, Helen Rand Parish, and Francis Sullivan, *The Only Way*. David M. Traboulay, *Columbus and Las Casas* Bartolome Las Casas, *Devastation*, 5. His work is generally used in two ways: first by Protestants to demonstrate the cruelty of the Spanish in the conquest of the New World and secondly to show the "other side" of the Amerindian point of view on the conquest. See Charles Gibson, *The Black Legend*. William S. Maltby, *The Black Legend*. Margaret Rich Greer, Walter Mignolo, and Maureen Quilligan, *Rereading the Black Legend*.

8. Edmundo O'Gorman, *The Invention of America*. "The only truly decisive point [about the discovery of America] was that Columbus had opened the way to lands inhabited by people in urgent need of God's word, so that they might have the opportunity and benefit of the holy sacraments before the world came to an end, an event Las Casas

cerned with the question of exactly what place Columbus discovered when he arrived in the New World and asks why Columbus's voyage is considered a success rather than a failure. After all, Columbus did not accomplish what he set out to do—he did not find Asia. O'Gorman argues that Las Casas played an integral role in the interpretation of Columbus's legacy as a success.[9] Las Casas's saw his own legacy as firmly connected to Columbus's discovery and the Christian duties of Spaniards in the New World. Las Casas argued that it was divine providence that led Columbus to the New World and that Columbus was an instrument of God's will. Since the New World had been found, Las Casas continued, it was now the duty of all Christians to convert the Amerindians and incorporate them into Christendom.

Las Casas was a devoted missionary as well as a theological jurist. His writings, especially *The Only Way* (1523), set out what became church policy for missionaries.[10] In that work, Las Casas provided guidelines for the ideal missionary. From Las Casas's perspective the missionary was not an instrument of colonial power and should not interfere with Amerindian sovereignty. The missionary should instead preach by being a "living example" of Christ, who had no desire for wealth or power and was modest and charitable.[11] Las Casas never suggested the New World should be abandoned by Europeans or the Amerindians' lands and states should be recognized as an equal to Europe. He argued instead for the continuing work of the church for the conversion of the Amerindians, but against the enslavement of Amerindians for European profit.

In order to demonstrate points of similarity between European "rationality" and Amerindians, Las Casas used Aristotle, antique authors such as Herodotus and Strabo, and church fathers such as Lactantius and Augustine. He marshaled these sources to support his position that Amerindians were to be treated as equals and as rational human beings. At stake in this issue of rationality was the very existence of Amerindians' souls. Beasts of burden were thought to be "irrational" and lack an eternal soul.

---

believed was imminent" (21).

9. "For Las Casas, Columbus was bound to fulfill the divine intentions which he was carrying out, independently of his own private objectives, so that the establishment of precisely what Columbus had wanted to do or what he thought he had done was a matter of no concern. The only important fact to be made clear was that God inspired in him the desire to undertake the voyage, and for this purpose there was no need to bicker about historical explanations; any one would do" (ibid., 20–21).

10. See Las Casas, Parish, and Sullivan, *The Only Way*. Las Casas, *Indian Freedom*.

11. See Las Casas, *The Only Way*.

Work Useful to Religion and the Humanities

If Amerindians were to be considered rational, i.e. ensouled, Las Casas argued it would be unchristian to enslave them.

Human sacrifice, practiced by the Aztecs and Incas, was considered to be the greatest evidence that Amerindians lacked rationality. In the *Defense of Human Sacrifice*, Las Casas used Aristotle's model of probable error to clarify exactly why the Amerindians cannot be held to be less than human for this practice.[12] Las Casas argued God can condemn Amerindians for this practice, as is God's right, but in the eyes of humanity, the Amerindians were simply doing what their culture had supported, from its laws, rulers, and most learned persons: "Even though the Indians cannot be excused in the sight of God for worshipping idols, *yet they can be excused completely in the sight of men* for two reasons. First, they are following a 'probable' error for, as the Philosopher [Aristotle] notes, *Topics*, Book I, something is said to be 'probable' which is approved by all men, either by the majority of wise men of by those whose wisdom has the greatest following."[13] Las Casas used Aristotle to argue against the number one reason given for Amerindian inferiority and barbarism: human sacrifice. Las Casas was also using Aristotle to argue against Aristotle, as it was Aristotle's understanding of natural slavery that Europeans drew on to justify the practice of slavery in the New World. Aristotle cut both ways in the New World, both for the land-holding Spanish *encomenderos* and the missionaries.[14] Las Casas's Aristotelian formulation supported his position that Amerindians could not be condemned by Europeans for their ignorance even as his opponents like Sepulveda used the Aristotelian understanding of barbarism to argue for the inherent inferiority of Amerindians. Las Casas argued Amerindian customs were within the norms of their culture and many of their customs exceeded Europeans' own cultural norms. Las Casas condemned Europeans for their mistreatment of the Indians in the strongest possible language before returning to his argument Amerindians were rational beings.

12. Las Casas, "*Defense*."
13. Las Casas, "Rationality," 187.
14. George Sanderlin writes "Aristotle was a two-edged sword. The Indians could be shown to measure up to his standards in many respects, yet Aristotle's underlying intention in his *Politics*, to justify Greek rule over non-Greek or 'barbarous' peoples, could tell against Las Casas. Indian customs such as human sacrifice and cannibalism might seem to invite a well-intentioned Spanish conquest, an undertaking of the 'white men's burden' of forcibly uplifting an 'inferior' race." See Sanderlin, ed., *Bartolome Las Casas: A Selection of His Writings*, 109.

The Comparative Method and Sacrifice in the New World

In many ways, Las Casas was a typical sixteenth-century missionary for whom God's providence was a primary concern. In order to demonstrate the presence of God in the New World, just as God had been present in the world before the revelation of Christ, he began a comparative project late in his life, comparing the Greeks and Romans to the Amerindians.[15] In the *Apologetica Historia*, Las Casas argued "They [the Amerindians] were equal to the Greeks and Romans. And in a good many customs they . . . surpass the Greeks and Romans."[16] Despite that bold assertion, the *Apologética Historia* contains only one chapter comparing Amerindians to the Greeks and Romans. The majority of the text was devoted to Las Casas's Aristotelian argument regarding the rationality of Amerindians. Las Casas began by describing the natural components of the New World such as the stars and the flora and fauna, in line with Aristotle's understanding that "natural causes" affected human development and contributed to human rationality. Consistent with those natural causes, which produced civilization and rational life in the Old World, the natural world created a rational environment in the New World. Therefore the greater part of Las Casas's book was devoted to the physical environment, the "six natural causes of good understanding—the influence of the stars, body make-up, climate, etc.," and the Aristotelian standards for civilized life.[17] Las Casas concluded the argument of the *Apologética* with Aristotle's four definitions of "barbarous" and the location of Amerindian culture within those definitions.

Las Casas carefully explained the four definitions of 'barbarous' in order to locate Amerindians on that spectrum. The first type of 'barbarism' related to acts of passion, "when men, forgetting the rules of reason"

---

15. In contrast to *Brevísma*, the *Apologética Historia* did not see the light of day outside the world of Catholic seminaries until 1875 and it received no scholarly attention even after that publication. The *Apologética Historia Sumaria* was written 1552 in Dominican Monastery in Puerto de Plata. Historian J.H. Elliott asserts that Las Casas's *Apologética Historia* "becomes a great essay in comparative cultural anthropology, in which the social and religious habits of Greeks, Romans, and Egyptians, ancient Gauls and ancient Britons, were examined alongside those of the Aztecs and the Incas, generally to the advantage of the latter . . ." Elliott, *The Old World*, 48. The exact date of the writing of the book and its construction is hotly debated. Hanke maintains Las Casas wrote the *Apologetica Historia* prior to the great debate with Sepulveda. O'Gorman believes that Las Casas wrote *Apologetica Historia* after the debate with Sepulveda and composed in 1555-1559.

16. Las Casas, *Indian Freedom*, 204.

17. Las Casas, *Witness*, 96.

commit acts "so savage that wild beasts . . . would not do worse."[18] The second definition of 'barbarous' was less broad and corresponded to the lack of written language within some cultures. This type of 'barbarous" being did not have "written speech that corresponds to their language as Latin does to ours."[19] The third type of 'barbarism' applied to peoples without social hierarchy, having no care for "law, right, nation, friendship, or the company of other men because of which they lack towns, councils, and cities, since they do not live socially."[20] These peoples, basically nomads, were undoubtedly the first type of Amerindian the Europeans encountered and by Aristotelian standards were the most 'barbarous.'

Lastly, the fourth type of 'barbarous' people were those who "lack true religion and the Christian faith" however "wise and prudent they may be as philosophers and statesmen."[21] This is a direct reference to the Greeks and Romans. Because Amerindians had never heard the gospel, "their infidelity does not bear the stigma of sin insofar as it consists of not possessing the faith of Jesus Christ," just as the Greeks and Romans could not possess faith in Jesus Christ.[22] In other words, these Amerindians found themselves in the same category as those pagans who lived before Christ who could not be damned because of their temporal location.[23] Amerindians could not be considered damned or less than human for the same reasons that Plato and Aristotle could not be considered irrational or damned.

Las Casas concluded the Amerindians were 'barbarous' only in the second and fourth senses. Even the second sense—lacking a written language—was somewhat flexible for Las Casas because the Amerindians possessed a kind of high art. "In the liberal and allied arts [they possess] a genius that awes everyone."[24] From Las Casas's point of view there was no justification for the enslavement and denigration of Amerindians: "Since all these Indian peoples . . . universally have good and natural intelligence . . .

---

18. See Ibid., x.
19. Ibid.
20. Ibid.
21. Ibid.
22. Ibid.

23. This is a very interesting theological move that protects some authors and their texts, such as Plato and Aristotle from being disregarded as non-Christian writings. See Lewis Hanke, *Aristotle*.

24. Las Casas, *Indian Freedom*, 203.

[they] can be drawn to and taught a complete and sound morality."[25] While Amerindians were outside the Christian world prior to the arrival of the Europeans, once Amerindians were 'found' they could be taught Christianity and brought into Christendom as brothers and moral equals, not as slaves and beasts of burden.

For Las Casas, who followed Aristotelian theological models, rationality was the primary marker of human existence. Rationality was considered God's gift to humans, the reason why humans had an immortal soul. Las Casas believed once Amerindians were compared with other "races," Europeans would see Amerindians were the same in the sight of God as Europeans. The *Apologética* provided the first attempt at that very comparison: "[T]he Indians [have] shown themselves to be very prudent peoples, with acute minds, having justly and prosperously governed their republics (so far as they could without faith and the knowledge of the true God), but *they have equaled many diverse races of the past and present*, much praised for government, way of life, and customs. And in following the rules of natural reason, they have even surpassed by not a little those who were the most prudent of all, such as the Greeks and Romans. This advantage ... will appear very clearly, if it please God, when the Indian races were compared with others."[26] [my emphasis] Las Casas argued once Amerindian customs had been compared with Greek and Roman customs, Amerindians would not be found wanting. This comparison would reveal that Amerindian were the equal to the 'races' of the European past, and so they should be seen as equals of Europeans by Europeans.

What is significant about Las Casas's texts is that Las Casas used various Aristotelian and classical comparisons to locate and understand Amerindian culture and life. Edward O'Gorman's critical introduction to Las Casas's *Apologética Historia* calls that work "a great essay in comparative cultural anthropology."[27]

---

25. Ibid., 204.

26. Sanderlin, ed., *Bartolome Las Casas: A Selection of His Writings*, 115.

27. Footnote to O'Gorman edition, 1967. Thomas and Carol Christensen Christensen, *The Discovery of America*, 243. The *Apologetica* is still is not translated into English, despite a critical appraisal by Edmundo O'Gorman published in 1967 and the interest in the era of Conquest stimulated by the 500th anniversary of the conquest. Also, few of the secondary sources on Bartolomé Las Casas deal with the *Apologética Historia Sumaria*. Because of its obscurity it has had relatively little intellectual life after its initial appearance in the 1550s.

Work Useful to Religion and the Humanities

Bartolomé Las Casas attempted to use European authorities to demonstrate Amerindian rationality and humanity. Las Casas's arguments for Europeans to recognize and acknowledge the basic humanity of Amerindians met with mixed results during his lifetime.[28] Las Casas advocated a scaled back conquest, focused on conversion rather than exploitation and slavery. A kinder, gentler conquest, if you will. He promoted a basic respect for Amerindian culture through the process of Christianization and colonization. While he did not win the debate with Sepulveda, he did make his mark on the hearts and minds of the missionaries who came after him. Las Casas was the first missionary to the New World to place Amerindians in European history through comparing "customs" to help Europeans understand the Amerindians. He was the first missionary-ethnographer.

BERNARDINO DE SAHAGÚN (1500–1590)

Like Las Casas, Bernardino de Sahagún struggled with the issues of conversion and questions about the origin of Amerindians and, like Las Casas, Sahagún wanted to provide guidance for future missionaries. Unlike Las Casas, however, Sahagún was focused on correcting Amerindian error rather than directing European behavior. As a result, Sahagún's comparisons were far more general than Las Casas' though he was also grounded in a strict Aristotelian framework.

Sahagún was a prolific writer. His most famous and well-known work is the *Historia Generale de las cosas de la Nueva España* written over thirty year period from 1530-1560, during his service as a missionary in the New World. This book is now collected in twelve volumes, known as the *Florentine Codex* (hereafter *FC*).[29] The *FC* was used by Sahagún's intended missionary audience as well as by other missionary-ethnographers, indigenous and Mestizo priests.[30]

---

28. Spain ended the practice of Indian slavery in 1542, though the practice was continued by the Portuguese. And this does not touch on the issue of African slavery. See Alan Gallay, *The Indian Slave Trade* and Colin A. Palmer, *Slaves of the White God*.

29. Bernardino de Sahagun, *General History of the Things of New Spain; Florentine Codex*. This codex has gone through various editions and also appears in Edward King Lord Kingsborough's *Antiquities of Mexico*, which made Sahagún's text available to many nineteenth-century scholars. For a further discussion of Sahagún's complete works, see Miguel Leon Portilla, *Bernardino De Sahagun*, 11-19.

30. See Miguel Leon Portilla, *Bernardino De Sahagun*. See also Serge Gruzinski, *The Mestizo Mind*.

The Comparative Method and Sacrifice in the New World

All of Sahagún's work was in the service of facilitating Amerindian conversion to Christianity. He wanted his texts to guide the process of conversion for Amerindians and gave careful attention to the roles he felt his brother missionaries should have in that process. Sahagún's goal was to better understand Amerindian culture as a tool in the conversion and colonization process. Sahagún writes: "I was ordered, by the holy command of my highest prelate, to write in the Mexican language that which seemed to me useful for the indoctrination, the propagation and perpetuation of the Christianization of these natives of New Spain, and as a help to the workers and ministers who indoctrinate them."[31] With the goal of assisting those who would work as missionaries among the Amerindians, Sahagún carefully documented those things he hoped would illuminate Amerindian culture for Europeans: "To preach against these matters [Amerindian religion and cultural practices], and even to know if they exist, it is needful to know how they practiced them in the times of their idolatry, for, through [our] lack of knowledge of this, they perform many idolatrous things in our presence without our understanding it."[32] By recognizing and understanding "idolatrous" practices and understanding how those rituals were performed, Europeans could not only begin the process of converting the Amerindians, they could also keep the newly converted from returning to their previous, un-Christian, ways. In his catalog of these idolatrous practices, Sahagún provided one of the few visions of Aztec culture in the early sixteenth-century that was based on first-hand accounts, Sahagún talked with natives about their beliefs and practices.[33] This act of preservation that has earned Sahagún the title "father of anthropology."[34]

---

31. Bernardino de Sahagun, *Florentine Codex*, 53.

32. Bernardino de Sahagun, *General History; Florentine Codex*, 45.

33. Sahagún's relationship to his sources must be thoroughly interrogated for inherent power dynamics and issues of presentation and representation. Sahagún's vision of Amerindians is somewhat conflicted. For example, he provides "eye-witness" accounts of the meeting between Montezuma and Cortes fifty years after the events. He interprets the signs and portents that the Aztecs told him were indicating to them the arrival of the Europeans and takes them as exactly that—signs and portent of the collapse of Aztec civilization rather than the other possibilities, such as a critique of Montezuma's reign, as Gruzinski suggests. Few scholars have really problematized the relationship between Sahagún and his informants. For a provocative discussion, see Serge Gruzinski, *The Conquest of Mexico*. See also Fernando Cervantes, *The Devil in the New World*.

34. Klor de Alva, *The Work of Bernardino De Sahagun*. See also Miguel Leon Portilla, *Bernardino De Sahagun*.

Work Useful to Religion and the Humanities

Sahagún's primary goals in writing his various text was to leave instructions for future missionaries that clearly demonstrated the error of Amerindian beliefs: "[T]he vanities they [Amerindians] believed regarding their lying Gods being understood, they may come more easily, through Gospel doctrine, to know the true God and to know that those they held as Gods are not Gods but lying Devils and deceivers."[35] In order to distinguish appropriate beliefs and practices from inappropriate ones, to distinguish lying Devils from the true God, Sahagún argued that Europeans must understand all native practices.

Understanding native practices served one purpose for Sahagún: conversion. However, Sahagún argued that conversion could not be secured without persuading Amerindians that their Gods were false—and that could not be done without careful investigation of those false deities. Sahagún defended this perspective by appealing to Augustine: "The divine Augustine did not consider it superfluous or vain to deal with the fictitious theology of the gentiles in the sixth Book of the City of God, because, as he says, the empty fictions and falsehoods which the gentiles held regarding their false Gods being known, [true believers] could easily make them understand that those were not Gods nor could they provide anything that would be beneficial to a rational being."[36] Rationality was central for Sahagún, as it was for Las Casas, but for Sahagún the emphasis was not to persuade Europeans that Amerindians were rational. Sahagún's purpose was to persuade Amerindians that their practices did not befit rational beings. Rather than emphasizing the rationality of Amerindians to Europeans, Sahagún emphasized the rationality of Amerindians to Amerindians. And the only way to make Amerindians understand their (pre-Christian) theology was not rational was to clearly understand that "fictitious theology."

As Sahagún points out, Amerindians were not the first to hold foolish or fictitious beliefs about the created world: "How foolish our forefathers, the gentiles, both Greek and Latin, had been in the understanding of created things is very clear from their own writings. From them it is evident to us what ridiculous fables they invented of the sun, the moon, some of the stars, water, land, fire, air and of the other created things. And, what is worse, they attributed divinity to them, and they worshipped them, made offerings, made sacrifices to them, and revered them as Gods."[37] Because

---

35. Bernardino de Sahagun, *General History; Florentine Codex*, 59.
36. Ibid.
37. Ibid., 67.

The Comparative Method and Sacrifice in the New World

Greek and Latin forefathers had demonstrated similar errors, Sahagún argued it was easy to understand how a people could maintain such beliefs and practices. The root of these foolish practices and ridiculous beliefs was to be found in the same two places for both Amerindians and Greek and Latin forefathers: original sin and "the cunning, . . . long-standing hatred of our adversary, Satan, who always inclines us toward vile, ridiculous and very culpable things."[38] Regardless of spatial (New World) or temporal (antiquity) location, all humanity suffers from two universal challenges: the flaw of original sin and the trial of Satan.

The same errors that Amerindians suffered could be seen in the gentiles, European Greek and Latin forefathers, "people of so much discretion and presumption."[39] From Sahagún's point of view then there was no reason for "one to marvel that similar things are found among these people [Amerindians] so innocent" and easily deceived.[40] This is the heart of Sahagún's comparative method. As Europeans knew and understood the erroneous practices and beliefs of the Greek and Latin forefathers, so Europeans should know and understand the erroneous practices and beliefs of the Amerindians.

In order to describe Amerindians practices and reveal their errors, Sahagún spent time with Amerindian informants and practiced a kind of sixteenth-century ethnography. It was his work with native informants makes Sahagún's texts as controversial today as they were during his era.[41] Sahagún's texts provide much of the material contemporary scholars use to reconstruct the pre-Columbian past because his is one of the only contact-era texts where a European made an effort to engage Amerindians about their culture, beliefs and practices.[42]

Converting native peoples took on even greater importance for Franciscan missionaries, especially during the early decades of the sixteenth-century when Sahagún's order was caught up in a millennial fever. Sahagún's brethren, the Spiritual Franciscans, found in the "poverty" of the Amerindian lifestyle the kind of religious practices they had hoped to inspire in

38. Ibid.
39. Ibid.
40 Ibid.
41. See Walden Browne, *Sahagun*. See also Miguel Leon Portilla, *Bernardino De Sahagun*.
42. See Klor de Alva, *The Work of Bernardino De Sahagun*, Miguel Leon Portilla, *Bernardino De Sahagun*. David Carrasco, *City of Sacrifice: The Aztec Empire and the Role of Violence in Civilization*.

Europe. In accord with their millennial expectations, the Spiritual Franciscans demonized Europe and saw Protestantism as the herald of the end of the world, with Luther as the anti-Christ. This made room for New World Amerindians to be a model of evangelical piety through their poverty. A "primitive church" like the church of Acts was possible in the New World, led by Franciscans and peopled by Christianity's newest, most Christ-like converts, the Amerindians.[43] It was considered necessary for all peoples of the world to hear the gospel in order to bring about Christ's return and the Spiritual Franciscans were preaching as aggressively as they could in order to hasten that return.

It is not clear how much Sahagún embraced the millennial beliefs of many of his contemporaries. However, he acknowledged the significance of the discovery of the New World for Christianity. The importance of the New World was found in the discovery of peoples who had been hidden from the word of God by the work of Satan: "It is certainly a matter of great wonderment that, for so many centuries, our Lord God has concealed a forest of so many idolatrous people whose luxuriant fruits only the demon harvested and holds hoarded in the infernal fire. Nor can I believe that the church of God would not be successful where the synagogue of Satan has had so much success, in accordance with that [phrase] of St. Paul's: 'Grace will abound where transgression abounded.'"[44] Whatever else was indicated by the discovery of Amerindians—the end of the world or vast European expansion—the possibilities for the conversion of Amerindians was great, and it was God's providence that provided Europeans with this great opportunity. Where the Devil had held such sway surely the church would be able to find even greater success. Sahagún wrote his texts with an eye to this success as well as an eye to the ways of the "demon" in order to better understand the world of the Amerindians. His was a scholastic humanistic approach, looking for a continual revelation of God's will—for example, the discovery of the New World—while at the same time understanding the importance of human action in God's work and the Devil's machinations.

Sahagún wrote about his apocalyptic hopes that the discovery of the Indies would lead to an easier path to Asia. He suspected the evangelization of Asia would be instrumental in bringing about the return of Christ. He wrote of the Augustinians who reached China in 1576: "It seems to me our Lord God finally opens the way that the Catholic Faith may enter in the

43. John Leddy Phelan, *The Millennial Kingdom*, 49.
44. Bernardino de Sahagun, *Florentine Codex*.

The Comparative Method and Sacrifice in the New World

Kingdom of China where there are very capable people of good breeding and wisdom. When the Church enters in those kingdoms and the Catholic Faith is established in them, I believe it will endure many years in that abode because in the islands and in this New Spain and Peru, it has done no more than pass through and still be on the way in order to communicate with those peoples in the regions of China."[45] In this passage, Sahagún showed his own support for the idea that the gospel must reach all parts of the world in order to bring about the return of Christ. While Sahagún was concerned that Christianity would not flourish in New Spain, he had some hope that the route through the New World to Asia would provide a pathway for the eventual conversion of the entire world.

Sahagún feared that Christianity would not flourish in New Spain. He witnessed a great deal of death and destruction of Amerindians peoples. He wrote "the people are becoming extinct with great rapidity, not so much from the bad treatment accorded them as the plagues God sends them."[46] He saw the plight of the natives—the continual threat of illness and the harsh treatment they received at the hands of the Spaniards—and despaired that his work as a missionary was in vain. By his own account he witnessed several outbreaks of smallpox and became so ill during one wave of the epidemic that he nearly died of small pox himself.[47]

Hidden in the *FC* are some very revealing passages. There Sahagún expressed his fear that the Catholic faith would fail to take hold in the New World; he worried about the "plagues" God had sent to the people of the New World, and he expressed his concerns about the roots of the religious practices of the peoples he had helped convert.[48] No where in the text is Sahagún's method for conversion and missionary work more clear than in these short passages. In these addenda were the early signs of the theological perspective that would fuel the method of Jesuit accommodation. For

---

45. Ibid., 100.

46. Ibid.

47. Ibid., lxx. "[I]n the year 1545, there was a very great and general plague in which the major portion of the people living in all this New Spain died. And at the time of this plague I resided in this city of Mexico, in the district of Tlatilulco. And I buried more than ten thousand bodies. And at the conclusion of the plague I contracted the sickness and was near death."

48. Walden Browne, *Sahagun*, 130-32. Browne argues these passages were fall back for Sahagún, a retreat to scholasticism in the face of the threat of failure in the New World but I see in them the shades of a new way of approaching the conversion of non-Christian peoples growing from Sahagún's sense of the overwhelming presence of New World peoples and the possibilities of God's purpose for native culture.

example, when he wrote about a yearly feast, Sahagún allowed that the Amerindians should keep the practice, albeit with strict European oversight: "the villages that enjoyed it [the feast] persuaded those provinces that they come as usual because they already had Tonantzin and Tocitzin and Telpochtli, who on the surface are like, or whom they made like, Saint Mary, Saint Ann, and Saint John the Evangelist or Baptist. And it is clear that, in the minds of the common people who come there, it is nothing other than the ancient custom. I now know that it comes from ancient custom. *And it is not my judgment that they should be denied either the coming or the offering, but it is my judgment that they be undeceived of the error from which they suffer, by giving them to understand,* on those days they come there, the ancient falsehood, and that it is not as in times of old."[49] [emphasis mine] The feast can be allowed to continue, but the people's belief must be directed toward the appropriate divinity (God the Father, the Trinity, the Virgin and the Saints). Sahagún's judgment that they should not be denied the feast and should be allowed to make their offerings, but that they should be "undeceived," gives an example of his particular method of comparison. By comparing the elements and correcting "errors," in belief and practice, Sahagún balanced Amerindian religion and Christianity.

Based on careful observation and comparison of elements of Amerindians' religion with Roman Catholicism, Sahagún could keep the hard-won converts in the embrace of the Catholic church and incorporate the practices from the pre-contact world within post-contact Christianity. This was possible only if those practices were not in direct conflict with Christian doctrine. Sahagún advocated this method of comparative missionizing for those preachers who were most capable of understanding the origins of Amerindian practice: "Preachers well versed in the language and the ancient customs which they [the natives] had, as well as in the Holy Writ..."[50] What is important in Sahagún's determination to allow some practices is his contention that the practice itself contained some kernels of Christianity. Because he believed this, he wanted the Amerindians "undeceived." Through careful explanation of those facets which were not Christian by a learned missionary in the Amerindians' language, the intent of the practice could be altered, could be made Christian. Sahagún advocated changing

---

49. Bernardino de Sahagun, *General History*, pp. 200.

50. Ibid., 1xx. This stems from a theological approach to works (humans working with grace can use free will for the good of creation) and emphasizes the inherent good to be found in creation.

The Comparative Method and Sacrifice in the New World

the way the people thought about the feast and offerings through education and catechism that rendered them sufficiently Christianized. As long as they were making their offering to God rather than to their old, false, deities, the feast was an approved practice in Sahagún's mind.

Sahagún was a missionary first and foremost. He was devoted to his vocation in every way. He embraced the expectations of his age and was both ethnocentric and Eurocentric. And yet, his motives were more complicated than those of a priest who longed for conversion and apocalypse. Sahagún was a missionary-ethnographer poised between a nascent form of Jesuit accommodation and the millennial Franciscans. He may have felt some despair that his work in the New World did not accomplish everything he had hoped. But in the end, he was resolutely devoted to a theological approach to New World-Old World comparison that saw the work of God in the New World through the lives of the natives he spent his life hoping to understand and convert.

Sahagún saw the Amerindians of New Spain possessing the same virtues and vices that were part and parcel of European life. His description of these moral and immoral persons highlights the Aristotelian emphasis on virtue: "All nations, however savage and decadent they have been, have set their eyes on other wise and strong in persuading, on men prominent for moral virtues, and on the skilled and the brave in warlike exercises, and more on those of their own generation than on those of others. There are so many examples of this among the Greeks, the Latins, the Spaniards, the French and the Italians that books are full of this subject."[51] While he does not give specific European examples, Sahagún alludes to the similarities between Amerindians and Europeans. Drawing on these implied comparisons, Sahagún offered a description of the "wise man." The text is both prescriptive and descriptive. Sahagún listed the attributes of wise men that he had known and observed in New Spain. These characteristics are universal—shared by all men, ancient and modern, European and Amerindian: "The wise man [is] exemplary. He possesses writings; he owns books. [He is] the tradition, the road; a leader of men, a rower, a companion, a bearer of responsibility, a guide."[52]

Sahagún also performed a similar task for the 'bad wise man:' "The bad wise man [is] a stupid physician, silly . . . A soothsayer, a deluder, he deceives, confounds, causes ills, leads into evil; he kills; he destroys people,

51. Ibid., 65.
52. Ibid., 29.

devastates lands, destroys by sorcery."[53] These descriptions give some insight into Sahagún's theological humanism. These men, good and bad, were capable of moral action in the world; they provided services for their community. Sahagún did not describe in detail the actions these men took, but he listed their attributes in much the same way that he made lists of words, body parts, and flora and fauna. In these descriptions humans, as the height of creation, demonstrate all their potential for good and evil.

When writing about human sacrifice, specifically, the sacrifice of children in the New World, Sahagún offered a clear perspective on his understanding of the role of God and the Devil in the world. He did not blame this "inhuman" cruelty on the people who sacrificed their children but rather on the Devil's actions in the world: "The blame for this cruel blindness perpetrated on these unfortunate children should not be imputed so much to the parents, who practiced it in shedding many tears and with great sorrow in their hearts, as to the most cruel hate of our most ancient enemy, Satan, who with most perverse cunning moved them to such an infernal deed. O Lord God, do justice upon this cruel enemy who does and would do so much evil! Lord, take from him all power to harm!"[54] Sahagún's prayer for God to do justice with Satan rather than either forgive or punish the Amerindian parents reveals his understanding of Satan as God's creature, capable of free will and intent on using Amerindians for his own purposes: "Consistent with [the passage] in the Holy Gospel which says, 'He who does evil detests light,' it is a very ancient practice of our adversary, the Devil, to seek hiding places in order to perform his works. Consistent with this, our enemy planted, in this land, a forest or thorny thicket filled with very dense brambles, to perform his works therefrom [sic] and to hide himself therein in order not to be discovered, even as do the wild beasts and the very poisonous serpents."[55] Satan hid in the New World. He had hidden from God and from God's agents, the church, in order to abuse the Amerindians and create them in his own Satanic image. However, the church was now able to "be successful where the synagogue of Satan has had so much success": the rocky soil of New Spain.

Bernardino de Sahagún was an early modern thinker. His thought reflects a blend of theology and humanism that combined Christianity and New World experiences to create a way of seeing the world in dialog across

53. Ibid., 29-30.
54. Ibid., 57-58.
55. Ibid.,. 58.

the oceans. This is what made him a missionary-ethnographer rather than just a missionary with some quaint interest in the culture of the people he hoped to convert.[56] Sahagún's texts were rich with descriptions of the inhabitants of New Spain and their lives therein. While his description often was coated with a veneer of theological disapproval and occasionally some apocalyptic hopes, Sahagún's text was nonetheless devoted to the scholastic understanding that all humans can work with grace within creation and toward salvation. Amerindians were not depraved persons, incapable of goodness, though neither were they people who possessed a greater moral or spiritual capacity. The people Sahagún described, catechized, and converted were imbued with the same talents, strengths, weaknesses, and foibles as the Spaniards. Correcting Amerindian error, in belief or in practice, could be accomplished by knowledgeable missionaries who carefully compared Amerindian beliefs and practices with known sources. Sahagún wanted to understand Amerindian culture so that he and future missionaries could identify those practices and beliefs that affected the spread of Christianity and conversion of the Amerindians.

JOSÉ DE ACOSTA (1540-1600)

Following in Las Casas's footsteps, José de Acosta was very interested in communicating Amerindian culture, beliefs, and practices to Europeans. And, following in Sahagún's footsteps, Acosta was concerned to examine the customs of the Amerindians in order to better demonstrate the error of their beliefs. Acosta expanded the justifications for studying Amerindians in order to revise European opinions of Amerindian culture and to allow Europeans to govern Amerindians more effectively. Like both Las Casas and Sahagún, Acosta structured his argument using Aristotelian categories. Unlike Las Casas, whose focus was rationality, Acosta focused on civilization. Acosta advocated allowing some of Amerindian culture to remain, especially those parts that contributed to the stability of Amerindian society and did not conflict with Christianity. And like both Las Casas and Sahagún, Acosta drew on comparisons with the Greeks and Romans to support his arguments for the appropriate method of European governance of the New

---

56. I will concede that Sahagun is not necessarily a Renaissance Humanist. However, I do not believe that he is the rigid, medieval thinker that Browne characterizes. His ambivalences complicate either characterization which is what makes his legacy both rich and controversial.

World colonies. However, more than either Sahagún or Las Casas, Acosta emphasized the role of the Devil and the possibility that Amerindians had been kept from God by the Devil. In fact, Acosta argued, the work of the Devil made Christianity's road in the New World a little smoother.

Acosta maintained that the first aim of studying the customs of Amerindians was to eradicate the "pernicious opinion" that Amerindians were lacking in humanity, rationality, and civilization.[57] Here Acosta continued the work of Las Casas, and hoped that Europeans would come to see that Amerindians had a culture that must be respected in its own right. Acosta bolstered his argument by comparing Amerindians with the Greeks and Romans: "In the wisest republics, such as those of the Romans and Athenians, we see signs of ignorance deserving of laughter; and, certainly, *if the republics of the Mexicans and Incas had been described in the times of the Romans or Greeks, their laws and government would be respected.*"[58] [emphasis mine] In other words, whatever errors Europeans perceive Amerindians to possess, those same errors can also be found in antique cultures. Furthermore, if the Romans or Greeks had "discovered" Amerindians, Amerindian culture and law would have been respected by those venerable empires of the European past with whom they share so much. By making this analogy Acosta put Amerindians on an equal footing with the "wisest republics" of the Greeks and Romans. Acosta encouraged Europeans to respect Amerindians in the process of incorporating them into Christendom.

Acosta's second objective in studying Amerindian culture was to argue for continuity within that culture. Acosta advocated that Amerindians should continue to practice aspects of their culture not directly in conflict with Christianity. Acosta argued that it was only through knowledge and understanding of Amerindian practices could Europeans govern well. "The other aim that can be achieved with knowledge of the laws and customs and polity of the Indians is to help them and rule them by those very laws, for in whatever does not contradict the law of Christ and his Holy Church, *they ought to be governed according to their statutes*, which are as it were their municipal laws." [59] Acosta maintained Amerindian laws and customs not directly contradicting Christian law should be allowed to remain in place. Using these indigenous laws would help maintain good relations between Spaniards and Amerindians. Disregarding or replacing their laws "cause

57. Jose de Acosta, *Historia.*, 329.
58. Ibid., 329-30.
59. Ibid., 330.

great harm" because it undermined Amerindian respect for the Spanish. At worst, disregard for Amerindian laws "makes us Spaniards abhorred as men who were and always have been their enemies in both good and evil."[60] Failure to acknowledge and respect Amerindian culture made Spaniards the Amerindian's enemies, regardless of whether the Spaniards do good or evil. Acosta argued there were many Amerindian beliefs and practices that were "worthy of admiration" and that these beliefs and practices show the Amerindians' "natural capacity" to receive good instruction and embrace Christianity.

Acosta was committed to an Aristotelian model of understanding the relationship between the natural world and the development of rationality, much as Sahagún and Las Casas were. Acosta began his work by examining the placement of the stars in heaven above the New World. He then explored the natural history and flora and fauna before he gave his account of where the Amerindians may have originated.[61] Finally, after this exploration of natural history and possible, non-biblical origins for Amerindians, Acosta arrived at the heart of his argument. He explained, following Aristotle, that there were three tiers of civilization and that Amerindians fit into the second tier because they possessed agrarian settlements and urban centers. The lowest tier of civilization does not have those essential elements of social life. However, the Amerindians were not equal to European civilization, the third tier, because they did not possess writing. This was important because the Amerindians possessed "history," but not in the same fashion as Europeans: "[The] remembrance of history, and of ancient times, can persist among men in one of three ways: either by letters and writing, as the Romans, Greeks, and Hebrews use, as well as many other nations; or by pictures, as have been used almost everywhere in the world (since, as was said in the second Nicene Council, pictures are a book for the illiterate); or by ciphers or characters, just as an arithmetical figure can stand for numbers one hundred, one thousand, and so on, without necessarily meaning the word *hundred* or *thousand*."[62] [emphasis in the text] According to Acosta, both Amerindian cultures and Asian cultures lacked the first form of writing—letters—but possessed the second and third forms of

60. Ibid., 330-31.

61. This is the structure of Sahagún's *Historia Generale de las cosas de la Nueva España* and Las Casas's *Apologetica Historia*. Acosta was an early advocate of migration as an explanation for the presence of Amerindians on the continent of the New World. See Ibid., 71-72.

62. Ibid., 331.

writing—pictures and arithmetical figures. Acosta spent a great deal of time explaining why, even though the Chinese have libraries that dwarfed European libraries of the time, the Chinese did not possess writing but rather pictures and ciphers only.[63] There is no question that Acosta was certain European culture was the height of civilized life. However, he admitted both Incas and Mexicans had a sophisticated combination of oral history and pictographic story-telling that preserved and conveyed their history to subsequent generations. Amerindians were a people without writing, but not a people without history. In order to establish the way Amerindians preserved and understood their history without writing, Acosta discussed the role of schools in Mexican education. He explained the role of scholarly discipline and rote memorization in the preservation of Mexican history.[64]

Acosta concluded that his *Natural and Moral History* was profitable for European readers: "[h]uman affairs resemble each other greatly, and some peoples learn from what has befallen others."[65] This was one of his purposes in writing *Natural and Moral History*. He wanted his book to be read as a "useful thing" for Europeans to understand what has transpired in the New World. "Knowledge of their [Amerindian] affairs tends to make them trust ours [European]" and in addition this knowledge would show Europeans how to treat Amerindians with respect.[66] This in turn would lead to the successful incorporation of Amerindians within European culture. Acosta's writing about Amerindian culture in Mexico and Peru have earned him the titles "Pliny of the New World," "protoethnographer," and "protoanthropologist."[67]

Acosta had great respect for the contribution of human imagination in his theological understanding of God's work in the world, particularly when he explained the existence of the New World. The problem of the

---

63. Ibid., 332.

64. Ibid., 341-41. "It is known that the Mexicans were very diligent in making boys commit those speeches and compositions to memory, and for this purpose they had schools, and as it were colleges or seminaries, where the old men taught the youths whom they had chosen to be rhetoricians and to practice the office of orators to learn famous orations, and commit them to memory word for word [. . .]." While Acosta writes that *this is known*, the example of Mexican schools is also found in Sahagún's General History of New Spain and this suggests Acosta had at least heard of Sahagún's text, if not had access to it himself. See also Elliott, *Spain*, 58-60.

65. Jose de Acosta, *Historia.*, 379.

66. Ibid., 380.

67. Claudio M Burgaleta, *Jose De Acosta*, 93.

existence of the New World plagued all the missionaries. In order to explain how the New World could exist without being mentioned in the Bible, Acosta turned to Seneca and the role of human imagination. Acosta believed it was possible that antique authors knew of the existence of the New World. Acosta argued human imagination was necessary to grasp the truth but not sufficient to produce correct understanding. "[I]t is not possible for human understanding to perceive and achieve the truth without making use of imagination."[68] But imagination must be combined with reason in order to produce understanding. Because, Acosta explained, imagination cannot go much farther than knowledge without becoming ridiculous. It was the combination of reason and imagination that allowed for antique authors to conceive of the New World. Acosta cites Seneca's *The Tragedy of Medea* as an example:

> After many long years will come
> a new and happy time,
> when our broad Ocean
> shall surpass its limits.
>
> A large land will be espied,
> another New World seen,
> when we sail the great deep
> that is now closed to us.[69]

With this example, Acosta believed that Seneca foresaw the New World. "[W]ith our own eyes we have seen this prophecy" fulfilled.[70] What Seneca had foreseen in his imagination had come to pass. Because Seneca did not have access to Christianity, Acosta reasoned one could not be certain Seneca recognized this imagined possibility as a true prophecy. Acosta concluded that Seneca "divined it with the kind of divination practiced by wise and perceptive men."[71] Acosta explained Seneca possessed imagination and was able to combine his imagination with the knowledge of his time to "foresee" the New World. Seneca knew there were many sea journeys being undertaken in his time and he also knew, via Aristotle, that there was another land opposite Europe. Combining this knowledge with his

---

68. Jose de Acosta, *Historia.*, 30.
69. Ibid., 42.
70. Ibid.
71. Ibid.

imagination, Acosta reasoned that Seneca was able to "divine" existence of the New World.

Regardless of where the Amerindians of the New World came from or whether Old World intellectuals foresaw their discovery, Acosta felt that since there were indeed people in the New World and had been for some time they must also have been imagined to exist (following both Aristotle and Anselm in their contention that that which we can imagine must be true). Amerindian existence had been imagined in the same way that the New World had been imagined. So, while unknown to Europeans until Columbus's discovery, Amerindians were not new or even beyond the realm of imagined possibility. Europeans had not possessed sufficient knowledge to recognize the prescient foreknowledge of the ancients. Acosta was concerned to show that Amerindian history and culture was valid and important for Europeans and possessed antique authority. Acosta maintained that there were "no peoples so barbaric that they do not have something worthy of praise" and that Amerindians certainly possessed institutions worthy of praise, regardless of their level of civilization or the possibility of European foreknowledge.[72]

Acosta concluded that even if his *Natural and Moral History* had "no other result than that of being an ordinary history and account of events that indeed took place," it, like all histories, "deserved to be received as useful thing."[73] Acosta felt that Europeans could learn from what had befallen Amerindians but he also felt that "there were no people so civilized and humane that they stand in need of no correction."[74] Acosta's work therefore had twin goals: to show what was good and worthy of admiration in Amerindian cultures and to educate Europeans with regard to Amerindian culture and their own culture. He accomplished these goals through careful comparison of antique and New World beliefs and practices.

Acosta's work provides accounts of the customs of two distinct Amerindian cultures found in Mexico and Peru. He broadly compared these groups of people (with no recognition of the varieties of culture in either location) with Greek, Roman and biblical accounts. He compared the degree of "error" between the Incas and Mexicans and suggested that these errors were similarly to the errors perpetrated by the Greeks and Romans: "[T]he Mexicans [are] more grievously in error and more pernicious than

72. Ibid., 379.
73. Ibid.
74. Ibid.

[. . .] the Incas [. . .]; for the greater part of their worship and idolatry was given to idols and not to natural phenomena in themselves, although they attributed these natural effect such as rain and flocks and war and procreation to the idols, just as the Greeks and Romans also set up idols to Phoebus and Mercury and Jupiter and Minerva and Mars . . ."[75] Like both Las Casas and Sahagún, Acosta was content to allude to the similarities without drawing sharp connections but the result was the same—the Old World provided a way to understand the new.

In the Incan and Mexican cultures Acosta saw the work of the Devil. The Devil was an important and lively character in Acosta's writings. Acosta understood the Devil to be a player in indigenous and Christian religions in the New World. Fernando Cervantes has argued that Acosta's understanding of diabolism complemented Amerindian beliefs about the dual natures of their deities and was thereby easily incorporated into the indigenous pantheon.[76] Indeed from Acosta's point of view, one of the reasons that Amerindians so readily adopted Christianity was "their very service and subjection to the Devil" who used mimicry of Christian sacraments as part of the indigenous religion.

In his insightful and provocative study of diabolism in the New World, Cervantes concludes that José de Acosta was a scholastic in all respects but one. Cervantes argues that Acosta rejected the scholastic understanding of the connection between grace and nature. Cervantes says that Acosta's "rejection of the Thomist concordance between nature and grace, *albeit not made explicit*, seems to be all important."[77] [emphasis mine] Cervantes maintains that this non-explicit distinction between nature and grace amounts to a distinction between the natural and supernatural in Acosta's understanding of Amerindian religion. In his argument, Cervantes contrasts Las Casas and Acosta. Cervantes maintains that Las Casas was able to "approach supernatural manifestations of Indian cultures from an essentially naturalistic standpoint" where Acosta implied a direct split between the supernatural and the natural world.[78] Cervantes argues that Acosta's understanding of the break between supernatural and natural worlds is so

75. Ibid., 259.

76. See Fernando Cervantes, *The Devil in the New World.*, especially chapter 2. This is further bolstered by arguments by Miguel León-Portilla about the dual nature not only of Mexica religion but all of Mexica art, philosophy and poetry. See Miguel Leon Portilla, *Aztec Thought*.

77. Fernando Cervantes, *The Devil in the New World*, 26.

78. Ibid., 31.

great that where Acosta wrote of the supernatural he seemed like a completely different writer than when he wrote of the natural world.[79]

The focal point of Cervantes' argument is the intersection between the natural world and the supernatural world. What Cervantes is establishing a theological connection between Jesuit missionary José de Acosta and Franciscan priests that is absent in later Jesuit and, particularly, indigenous priests. The connection Cervantes wants to see is grounded in what he defines as "early modern diabolism" which he sees directly connected to "the Franciscan rejection of Aristotelian naturalism."[80] This rejection results in an embrace of theological nominalism and a "growing acceptance of the moral system of the ten commandments in early modern Christianity in the New World."[81] According to Cervantes, Acosta and the New World Franciscans who ran the Inquisition in Mexico replaced a scholastic-Aristotelian naturalism with an Augustinian emphasis on human depravity and original sin. The reason that Acosta would reject Aristotelian naturalism is the indigenous practice of human sacrifice. The problem of human sacrifice and how to interpret and understand it troubled all chroniclers of the New World and continues to be a topic of scholarly interest and exploration.[82] Acosta was no exception and this particular issue occupied a significant portion of his description of the "idolatry" of the Mexicans.[83]

Cervantes sees Acosta employing the scholastic synthesis of nature and grace as well as being especially interested in exploring the possibilities of knowledge based on experience until Acosta confronts religion. Then, Cervantes maintains, Acosta becomes ambivalent about the relationship between natural and supernatural: "As soon as he entered the field of religion proper Acosta seemed to join the nominalist camp and all his insistence on empirical knowledge and analysis was brought to a complete standstill."[84] Las Casas and Acosta were very similar writers and their approach is grounded in scholastic humanism. However, it is pos-

---

79. See Ibid., 26. "Indeed, the contrast between his treatment of what he regarded as natural and his analysis of what he thought to belong to the 'supernatural' sphere in the cultures of American is so striking that, at first sight, it is hard to believe that they were constructs of the same mind."

80. Ibid.

81. Ibid., 24.

82. For contemporary contextualization, see Miguel Leon Portilla, *Aztec Thought*, and especially David Carrasco, *City of Sacrifice*.

83. See Jose de Acosta, *Historia.*, especially book 5, chapters 20-27, pp. 293-311.

84. Fernando Cervantes, *The Devil in the New World*, 27.

sible, while acknowledging Cervantes contribution to our understanding of diabolism in the New World particularly within the indigenous context, to see Acosta's position another way. Acosta's understanding of diabolism was an extension of his understanding of the relationship between God and the Devil and that understanding was grounded in a scholastic, humanistic worldview.

Aquinas maintained that the Devil was a creature—God's creation rather than an independent entity.[85] While moral evil cannot be willed by God, Aquinas saw God permitting moral evil for the sake of good. However, the scholastic synthesis of nature and grace holds that nature (human or angelic) will always work with grace for the good of God's creation. In other words, human nature is always striving towards God and salvation. Even in the worst events, such as human sacrifice, Acosta saw the Devil mimicking holy sacraments. It was possible for grace to pull those events into accord with God's will for good.[86] It was consistent with this position that God is able to use the acts of his creature, Satan, for the greater good of the inhabitants of the New World. Acosta maintained that mimetic practices introduced by the Devil, however horrific those practices may have been, made the conversion of the Amerindians even easier as they were prepared for the mystery of the eucharist through Satan's imitation of that practice.

The way Acosta saw the Devil in the New World is similar to Sahagún's vision of the Devil's actions in the New World. The Devil kept the Amerindians for himself and used them to mock God. Acosta reasoned that the Devil came to the New World because he had been driven out of the rest of the (Christian) world: "the Devil retires to the remote places and reigns in that other part of the world. . . ."[87] From Acosta's point of view, during his reign in the New World the Devil kept the Amerindians from God and led them into two kinds of evil. First, he made them deny God. Second, the Devil's goal is "to make man subject to something lower than himself, for all creatures are inferior to the rational creature [by which Acosta means humans], and the Devil, although in nature he is superior to man, in estate is much inferior, because man even in this life is capable of divine and eternal

---

85. See Frederick Charles Copleston, *Aquinas*, 146. "For sheer evil is an impossibility. Aquinas does not mean to deny the existence of Satan. But for him Satan is not an ultimate being at all, but a creature. Created good, he remains good, if considered simply as a being."

86. "[E]vil indicates the absence of good. But not every absence of good is evil." Saint Thomas Aquinas, *Introduction*, 268.

87. Jose de Acosta, *Historia.*, 254.

life. And so . . . God is dishonored and man destroyed, and in both cases the proud and envious Devil is well content."[88] In this New World, the Devil had succeeded in both his goals from Acosta's perspective, until Europeans came to lead Amerindians out of the darkness of idolatry and into the light of Christianity.

The primary form of idolatry the Devil encouraged in Amerindians was sacrifice. Acosta defines three types of sacrifices that the Devil "taught the heathen for his worship."[89] These were sacrifices of insentient things, animals and men: "But what is most painful about the unhappy lot of these wretched people is that vassalage that they paid to the Devil, sacrificing men to him, who are made in the image for God and are created to enjoy God. As has been said above, in many nations they had the custom of killing, to accompany their dead, the persons who had been most pleasing to them and who they imagined could best serve them in the other life."[90] Acosta did not resort to the theological language of human depravity, original sin, irrationality, or inhumanity. Acosta concluded his discussion of the variety of human sacrifices and blood sacrifices performed by Amerindians in peace and war: "an infinite amount of human blood was shed in every way in honor of Satan."[91] Acosta did not see sacrifice as a question of the depravity of human nature or the weakness of humanity. He blamed Satan and saw sacrifice as Satan's "work" to be reformed through grace and nature into salvation for the Amerindians. In this way he followed Sahagún's assessment that it was Satan who should bear the blame for human sacrifice rather than the Amerindians.

Acosta addressed the sacrifice of children, too, and compared this to sacrifices from the Old Testament, specifically the "barbarous nations of the Chanaanites [sic] and Jebusites and the others written about in the Book of Wisdom."[92] He referred to the sacrifice King Moab made "when he sacrificed his firstborn son upon the wall in the sight of the Israelites."[93] Claudio Burgaleta, in a recent biography of Acosta, argues that Acosta was demonstrating that these kinds of "errors" and idolatries had been practiced by the great empires of classical antiquity as well as by the Hebrews.

88. Ibid., 255.
89. Ibid., 288.
90. Ibid., 291.
91. Ibid., 297.
92. Ibid., 292.
93. Ibid.

The Comparative Method and Sacrifice in the New World

Acosta's implication is that if the Hebrews, God's chosen people, had been idolatrous and had not been rejected by God then the Amerindians were not to be rejected by God. If God does not reject these peoples who were the Europeans to reject them?[94]

Acosta continued his discussion of ways the Devil mimicked the holy church. "And it is certainly worth noting that the Devil, after his fashion, has also introduced a trinity into idolatry,"[95] as well as the feast of corpus Christi, communion, last rites, and confession.[96] Acosta concluded Book V of *Natural and Moral History* and his accounts of Amerindian "idolatry" with the hope that his book would serve Europeans and God. Knowledge of Amerindian culture and religious practices would help Spaniards understand the Amerindians as well as the Devil's methods. Acosta's work also served to remind Spaniards of the glorious nature of God's laws and to be thankful for the love of God. Lastly, he encouraged Spaniards to pray for those who "still persist on the path to perdition."[97] In this way, Acosta wanted to "move human hearts to work for the salvation" of the Amerindians.[98]

In his conclusion to Book V, Acosta wrote that the things he has recounted were idolatries instigated by the Devil for his own purposes in the New World: "for on the one hand he wants to imitate God and compete with him and his Holy Law and on the other he mixes in an infinite number of vanities and filth, and even cruelties, since *it is his role to wreck havoc on everything good and corrupt it.*"[99] [emphasis mine] Acosta sees the Devil's deceptions, mimicries and cruelties as the part the Devil plays in God's creation. Cervantes sees Acosta following scholasticism right up to this point. Then, faced with the Devil, Cervantes sees Acosta retreat to a less modern, more medieval stance.[100] I am arguing that Acosta's vision was in accord

---

94. Claudio M Burgaleta, *Jose De Acosta*, 97-98. "Acosta's subtext is that if Israel was idolatrous and yet not rejected by God, then neither should the Spaniards reject the native peoples of the Americas on the grounds that they were depraved and idolatrous nations."

95. Jose de Acosta, *Historia.*, 315.

96. Ibid., 301-18.

97. Ibid., 327-28.

98. Claudio M Burgaleta, *Jose De Acosta*.

99. Jose de Acosta, *Historia.*, 327.

100. Fernando Cervantes, *The Devil in the New World*, 30. "Since, however, such similarities [corpus Christi feast for Huitzilopochtli, baptism, marriage, confession and sacerdotal unction] were a clear proof of the demonic nature of Indian religions, Acosta chose to overlook the chastity of the 'monasteries' and the asceticism of the 'penitential'

with scholastic, humanistic thought of the period. In the conclusion of the work, Acosta writes:

> It was of no little help that the Indians received the Law of Christ so willingly, owing to the great subjection in which they are held by their kings and lords. *And their very service and subjection to the Devil and his tyrannies, and his heavy yoke, created an excellent opportunity for Divine Wisdom, which takes advantage of bad things to turn them into good, and makes its own good out of other's evil, with which it had nothing to do* . . . Hence Christ's law seemed to them, and still seems, just, easy, pure, good, equitable, and wholly full of good things. *And what is difficult in our religion*, that is, having to believe such lofty and sovereign mysteries, *was made much easier among them because the Devil had told them other things that are much more difficult*; and the same things he stole from our Gospel law, such as its style of Communion and Confession, worship of the three in one, and other such matters, helped the Indians against the enemy's will to receive in truth the things that they received as lies [my emphasis].[101]

This conclusion, that the works of the Devil paved the way for the conversion of the Amerindians, was fully in accord with the scholastic understanding of the role of the Devil as a creature of God, a creature whose acts, however cruel and deceitful, could be used by God for the good of creation.

The issue of human sacrifice challenged all missionaries. Comparing other accounts of sacrifice from antiquity and the Hebrew Bible, Acosta found a way to understand the practice. Through this understanding he advised Europeans on interacting with and governing Amerindians. Like both Las Casas and Sahagún, Acosta was also a (Christian) ethnographer. All three of these missionaries shared aims that required that they "understand" the culture they were trying to Christianize. All three grounded that understanding in the practice of comparison to establish points of similarity between Europeans and Amerindians. Once these points of similarity were established, the missionaries then drew theological conclusions about particular Amerindian beliefs and practices and guided New World peoples into Christendom.

---

practices and to stress that pagan religious ceremonies were invariably mixed with all types of 'abominations' that inverted and perverted the natural order." (30)

101. Jose de Acosta, *Historia*, 447.

CONCLUSION

Las Casas, Sahagún, and Acosta were the first missionary-ethnographers to make any effort to catalog the practices of Amerindians and the first to engage in cultural comparison in the New World. Their works have been consulted since they were written and remain provocative today. Las Casas's work is controversial because of the ways his text has been understood to represent the "reality" of the Amerindian condition during the early years of European/Amerindian contact. Sahagún's work may be the first example of the practice of anthropology or the last gasp of medievalism.[102] Acosta's work is hotly debated because of his understanding of the role of the Devil in the religious practices in the New World.

One possible reason for some of the similarities found in Sahagún, Las Casas and Acosta could be found in their similar education. All three were educated in Spain at the University of Salamanca. Salamanca was the leading educational institution of European religious through the sixteenth- and seventeenth- centuries.[103] This educational background would have given these scholars a similar mentalité and provided each with the Aristotelian categories and mindset.[104] This similarity in education may also account for the similarities in their theological and comparative approaches to Amerindians. Bernardino de Sahagún, Bartolomé Las Casas, and José de Acosta were dedicated humanists, especially with regard to the treatment and conversion of Amerindians.

The University of Salamanca in Spain was the finest school and premiere cultural center of Europe during the sixteenth- and seventeenth-centuries. Philosophy was the crowning discipline of Salamanca and many of the finest European intellectuals were educated there. According to Leon-Portilla's recent biography of Sahagún, many subject areas were covered in Sahagún's education such as "medicine, mathematics, astronomy, music, moral theology, and theology."[105] Students educated at Salamanca were

---

102. Walden Browne, in his provocative study of Sahagún's legacy, argues that scholasticism is a remnant of a medieval worldview forced on all religious thinkers of the early modern period. He sees Sahagún as a combination of this medieval worldview and the beginning of a modern worldview. Browne argues scholasticism is a "medieval way of knowing" that is dying out and being replaced with a 'modern' way of knowing that Sahagún is on the cusp of developing. Walden Browne, *Sahagun*.

103. Grice-Hutchinson, *The School of Salamanca*.

104. Portilla, *Bernardino De Sahagun*. Paul Oskar Kristeller, *Medieval Aspects*.

105. Portilla, *Bernardino De Sahagun*, 38.

expected to know Greek, Hebrew and Latin and studied antique authors.[106] The foundation of the education at Salamanca was Renaissance humanism.

Renaissance humanism had three primary concerns. First was a reverence for and intense focus on classical antiquity. Second was an emphasis on humanistic education with special attention to history. Humanities were thought to provide people with ideals toward which to aspire. For Christian humanists, these ideals needed to be both classical and Christian, but as Christianity had been incorporating classical elements since its birth, missionary-ethnographers rose to this challenge ably. Lastly, renaissance humanism placed humanity at the center of creation. This locale highlights individuality, potential, and, above all, free will.[107]

Grounded in their humanistic educational experiences, Las Casas, Sahagún, and Acosta compared Amerindians with the Greeks and Romans and concluded, though the Amerindians may have been deceived and led

---

106. There is some debate about the influence of early modern humanism at the University of Salamanca. Walden Browne argues the University of Salamanca was steeped in the "medieval worldview" of the high middle ages. He sees Sahagún as a scholastic but rejects the idea that Sahagún was a kind of Christian humanist. (pp. 79-80) However, Sahagún emphasized rhetoric, moral philosophy and the importance of classical thought and learning. These were all markers of humanism and were also particularly consistent with scholasticism, which embraces a strong sense of human agency in the maintenance of the world. Scholastic theology is flexible in order to incorporate humanity's free will God's work through grace. This approach is very different from the more Augustinian understanding of human depravity. These three missionary-ethnographers were proponents of a theological vision of grace wherein grace permits human free will to cooperate in salvation.

Browne argues that "Sahagún was not a humanist because he was 'humane' or brought some so-called humanist philosophy to bear on his missionary endeavors; he was a missionary whose linguistic, humanistic formation became one of the important features of how he carried out his work. In this very limited sense of the word, 'humanism' does not appear to be an appropriate term to use for Sahagún." (p. 80) The majority of Browne's understanding of the Scholastic and Medieval theological worldview comes from Erwin Panofsky, *Gothic Architecture and Scholasticism*. This significantly weakens Browne's argument because he disregards contemporary scholarship on historical theology, especially new understandings of scholastic theological humanism which come primarily from scholarship on the Society of Jesus. Browne fails to recognize the importance of Christian humanism in scholastic thought. Many Christian humanists reject scholasticism but many scholastics embraced humanism. See Portilla, *Bernardino De Sahagun*. Browne does not give credit to the theological conflicts present in during the contact era. What is crucial to my argument regarding missionaries and theology is that theology is a living discipline not a static structure. See Kristeller, *Medieval Aspects*, O'Malley, *The First Jesuits*.

107. For a thorough discussion of those three points, see Bard Thompson, *Humanists and Reformers*, 205-28.

into error, they were more than capable of being included in the Christian European world. Their purposes were to facilitate the process of conversion within the colonial enterprise and to bring Amerindians into the European world. All three of these missionaries spent their lives with Amerindians and their struggles and questions grew out of their immediate colonial concerns. By the eighteenth-century, this method of comparison would shift from a method of understanding the Amerindians to a method of understanding Europeans.

3

The Comparative Method and Reflections of Antiquity

I have not limited myself to learning the characteristics of the Indian and informing myself about their customs and practices, I have sought in these practices and customs, vestiges of the most remote antiquity.

JOSEPH-FRANCOIS LAFITAU
Moeurs Des Sauvages Ameriquains

BY THE BEGINNING OF the eighteenth century the Society of Jesus had missions established in most parts of the world. Jesuits spent their time in these missions learning native languages, teaching, preaching conversion to their indigenous communities, and writing about their experiences. Like many of his brothers, Jesuit Joseph François Lafitau (1681–1746) was interested in the salvation of Amerindians and Europeans. Like the missionary-ethnographers before him, Lafitau was acutely interested in comparing Amerindians with what he knew from antiquity. But Lafitau went a step further than his predecessors. Las Casas, Sahagún, and Acosta all compared Amerindians with Greek and Romans to find ways that Amerindians were like those European predecessors. Lafitau explored "the vestiges of the most remote antiquity" by looking at antiquity through comparison with Amerindian beliefs and practices in order see the ways in which European predecessors were similar to Amerindians. By making this

The Comparative Method and Reflections of Antiquity

two-way comparison—Amerindians are like Europeans, Europeans are like Amerindians—Lafitau was able to see antiquity come to life in Amerindian practices: in order to see what Plato had described, all one had to do was look in the right place—the New World.

In this chapter, I will argue Lafitau constructed his comparisons of European and Amerindian cultures in order to demonstrate the religious unity of all humanity, regardless of spatial (New World) or temporal (antiquity) location. By comparing ancient and Amerindian peoples, Lafitau was able to make an argument for a single, Christian origin for religion. His goal was not only to show Europeans the Amerindians were like Europeans, but also to demonstrate Amerindians were the direct descendents of the "barbarians" of antiquity. Once Lafitau established the connection between Amerindians and the ancient Greeks, he could argue the Amerindians provided a view into the practices of "pagans" as described by antique authors. Amerindians were living those practices and beliefs the peoples of pre-Christian Europe had lived.

Lafitau's comparative method involved reading antique and New World texts in order to compare Amerindians and ancients. These comparisons were designed to prove that Amerindians were descended from "barbarians" described by Greek and Roman authors. Lafitau's method was grounded in a process of comparing discrete elements from various myths with equally discrete elements of biblical narratives. This process involved comparing components from myths from around the world (India, North America, Greece) with biblical stories. The story I will focus on in this chapter is the story of Adam, Eve, Cain, and Abel from the book of Genesis. Based on the similarities between the stories, Lafitau argued his comparison demonstrated the Christian God is the originator of all religion.

The second step in Lafitau's system was to establish genealogical connections between Amerindians (who lived in the New World and therefore had no knowledge of Christ) and Greeks and Romans (who lived before the revelation of Christ). He did this in order to demonstrate Amerindians were the descendents of the "barbarians" of antiquity and living as the barbarians described in antique texts. Amerindian practice and beliefs allowed Lafitau to witness and explain practices and beliefs of the ancients. This is precisely what Lafitau's system adds to the practice of comparison: he uses Amerindian culture to look at, to see in living culture, peoples described in antique sources. Las Casas, Sahagún and Acosta all compared Amerindian customs with antique accounts to understand Amerindian customs. Lafitau compared Amerindian customs with antique customs to understand Amerindian customs but also to understand antique customs. This two-way vision allowed Lafitau to claim to clearly see both antique customs and Amerindian customs.

In order to explain Lafitau's method of comparison, I will first explore how he established the religious unity of all humanity. He argued "religion" was universal and had originated with the God of Christianity: the God of revelation, who inscribed true religion on the hearts of humanity at the beginning of time. Lafitau argued religion had two universal practices that gave evidence of its existence across time: sacrifice and belief in the soul. I will explore his analysis of myths in relation to the Bible and show the components of his comparative method. Then I will explore the second step of Lafitau's system by explicating his views of the practices of burial and "warrior partners" (*athenrosera*) in antiquity and the New World. Through an examination of Lafitau's comparisons, I will show the way his system illuminated the antique past and saw it resurrected in the New World.

Building on the early comparative efforts of the missionary-ethnographers Bernardino de Sahagún, Bartolomé Las Casas, and José de Acosta, Lafitau added a new dimension to the colonial project of understanding New World inhabitants and their religion. Lafitau's additional insight lay in the power of the practices of the Amerindians to clarify antique texts and educate Europeans about not only Amerindian culture but also the antique past. While mirroring much of the material collected and produced by Sahagún, Las Casas, and Acosta, Lafitau added to their perspective by not only showing there were similarities between Amerindian practices and antique and biblical texts, but also demonstrating those similarities could educate Europeans about their past.[1] Through his unique method of comparison, Lafitau used Amerindian, Greek, and Roman texts to observe history. Through the lens provided by those "practices and customs" of the Amerindians, Lafitau saw the past.

---

1. In the critical introduction to *Moeurs*, William Fenton notes that Lafitau cites Acosta's work *Moral and Natural History* "frequently and accurately." Joseph-Francois Lafitau, *Moeurs*, 32.

The Comparative Method and Reflections of Antiquity

LIFE AND WORKS OF JOSEPH FRANÇOIS LAFITAU (1681-1746)

Joseph- François Lafitau was born in Bordeaux in 1681. He joined the Society of Jesus in 1696. Like many Jesuits of this era, he spent his early years in the order teaching in Jesuit schools and pursuing his own education. After completing his education, Lafitau taught through the first ten years of his formation at College Louis Le Grande.[2] In 1711 Lafitau returned to Bordeaux to become professor of Rhetoric at the College of Bordeaux. Also during that year, he asked the Father General of the Society of Jesus Michelangelo Tamburini to send him to New France to serve as a missionary.[3]

In 1712 Lafitau's request was granted and he departed for New France. He went to Sault St. Louis, on the south shore of the St. Lawrence river in what is now northeast Canada. Lafitau was there for six years as a missionary to the Iroquois. It was probably during this time Lafitau mastered the Iroquois language. Lafitau learned local languages and acquired local knowledge at the Sault St. Louis mission; he was not a particularly biographical writer. He left very few hints about his personal life and spirituality. He said even less about what he thought about his situation or neophyte Christians living at the mission. He also did not reveal the identities of his living informants.[4] Possibly this is because, while it is evident Lafitau spoke some Iroquois, he also made use of other sources about the region,

---

2. An early modern Jesuit would have spent two years in rigorous training using Ignatius of Loyola's *Spiritual Exercises*. After successfully completing that segment of his formation, he then would have spent two years studying the "ancient classics." From that point the young Jesuit would begin a three year course in philosophy that encompassed logic, epistemology, ontology, ethics, cosmology, theodicy, natural science and mathematics. At this point, the Jesuit was seven years into his training and usually received his first teaching appointment. Depending on the demand for teachers for the various Jesuit schools, a novice would spend from one to five years in this teaching position. After a tenure as teacher, the Jesuit began to study theology, specifically scholastic theology, for four years. He studied apologetics, canon law, dogmatic and moral theology, scripture, and ecclesiastical history. Sometime during this time of study, usually around the third year, the Jesuit was ordained as a full priest. After that ordination he had one year of spiritual formation and then was sent into the field as a missionary, educator, diplomat, etc., where he often finished his life. See Martin, *The Jesuit Mind*; and Jacobsen, *Educational Foundations*.

3. Michelangelo Tamburini was Superior General of the Society of Jesus from 31 Jan 1706—28 Feb 1730.

4. Lafitau, *Moeurs*, xxxiii. "[T]here is no hint as to how Lafitau did his field work or who were his other informants."

carefully "cribbing" from Sagard and Champlain.[5] Lafitau was most noted for his discovery of North American Ginseng in the forest bordering the St. Lawrence river.[6] It was this discovery that put Lafitau on the eighteenth-century intellectual map.[7]

After five years at the Sault Saint. Louis mission, Lafitau returned to France. He had two goals for his time in France. The first was to acquire permission to move the mission in search of better soil and resources and second was to procure an order to stop the sale of alcohol to Amerindians. This issue was a concern to all of the missionaries to the Sault Saint Louis mission since the early years of the mission.[8] Lafitau's only contribution to the *Jesuit Relations*, a multi-volume collection of letters, mission reports, and Society of Jesus activities in the New World, was a short letter concerning the sale of alcohol to the Amerindians.[9] This is the only document Lafitau wrote during his missionary life in the New World. His other works were all completed after his final return to France in 1729.

What is clear from Lafitau's relation was the life of the mission was seriously impaired by the Amerindians' use and abuse of alcohol and by European complicity through the alcohol trade. Amerindians used alcohol

---

5. Snow, *The Iroquois*, 40. "Joseph Lafitau wrote the most detailed description [of a longhouse] in 1724. Historians have often treated these [Sagard's description and Champlain's description of a longhouse] as independent sources, but careful reading of Sagard reveals he cribbed from Champlain and, Lafitau cribbed from both of them."

6. Lafitau, *Moeurs*, xxxiii.

7. Ibid.

8. The alcohol problem in the Canadian missions haunted the *Jesuit Relations* through the eighteenth-century. In 1702, Father Étienne de Carheil complained that the missions were over-run with troubles caused by the brandy trade. He wrote that missions "were reduced to such an extremity that we can no longer maintain them against an infinite multitude of evil acts—acts of brutality and violence; of injustice and impiety; of lewd and shameless conduct; of contempt and insults. To such acts the infamous and baleful trade in brandy gives rise everywhere, among all the nations up here, —where it is carried out by going from village to village, and by roving over the lakes with a prodigious quantity of brandy in barrels, without any restraint." Carheil implored the governor of the region to represent his case to the king and hoped to stem the alcohol trade in the colony. He continued that he was so full of despair that "there is no other step to take than to leave our missions and abandon them to the brandy traders, so that they may establish therein the domain of their trade, of drunkenness, and of immorality" (191). Carheil implored the governor to secure an edict from the King to stop the alcohol trade to "save our missions and to support the Establishment of Religion" in order to secure the mission and surrounding areas for France. Jesuits, *The Jesuit Relations and Allied Documents*, vol. 66, x–xx.

9. Lafitau, "Memorial," x.

to seek visions and have shamanistic experiences. Jesuits saw themselves in direct competition with shamans for religious authority. Lafitau's mission to France to procure the "memorial" to stop the alcohol trade was certainly informed not only by a concern for Amerindians but also out of a concern for the success of Jesuit mission in Sault Saint Louis and throughout the French territories.[10] The concern the French were losing the moral high ground, as well as jeopardizing the colonies, was a main feature of Jesuit writing of the period and Lafitau is no exception to this rule.[11]

From 1717 to 1727 Lafitau was in France, researching and writing *Moeurs*. He made occasional visits to Rome to argue for the relocation of the Sault Saint Louis mission to better farm land but his primary work in France was on his book. *Moeurs* was first published in 1724. In 1727 Lafitau returned to New France as Superior of the Sault Saint Louis mission. But he was only there for two years before he returned to France. There he began preparation of his second work, *Histoire des descouvertes et des conquetes des Portugais dans le Nouveau-Monde*, which was published in 1734.[12] He did not return to the New World again, and spent the rest of his life writing about the customs of the Amerindians and working in the Paris mission.

Moeurs was relatively well-received in the intellectual world of eighteenth-century Paris. It was favorably reviewed in the *Journal de Trevoux*, a Jesuit literary journal published chiefly for the lettered class in France.[13] The reviews published in the journal were printed anonymously and provide an insight into the interaction between the Society of Jesus and the intellectual world of Paris.[14] It is important to understand that Lafitau and other Parisian Jesuits were involved in both the intellectual life of the church and with

10. Morrison, *The Embattled Northeast*: "The missionaries also found alcohol a source of embarrassment, for the destructive liquor traffic belied French moral superiority and thus made the priests aware that French culture itself obstructed the conversion of the Abenaki. In opposing the liquor trade, the Jesuits eventually learned that they had to deal with the political implications of religious alliance" (93).

11. Jaenen, *Friend and Foe*: "A more recent rationalization of Amerindian drinking patterns maintain that the Iroquoian groups in particular accepted alcohol with eagerness, not for its taste, but to produce intoxication as a means of stimulating vision experiences which were highly regarded in the native cultures" (114).

12. Lafitau, *Histoire*.

13. *Memoires Pour L'histoire Des Sciences & Des Beaux Arts*.

14. O'Keefe, *Contemporary Reactions*: "Since the articles in the Journal de Trévoux are not signed it is only from other sources that it is possible to identify the authors. Throughout the entire history of the journal there is a distinct note of anonymity which is always present; this precluded even the listing of the members of the editorial board" (7).

"secular" intellectuals of their day. Lafitau would have expected his work to be read by other members of the order interested in the development of religion as well as by his non-religious peers.[15]

Moeurs is Lafitau's best known work. In this chapter, I focus on the method Lafitau employed to establish his system for understanding Amerindian religion in comparison with antique authors. Lafitau's method consists of close reading of antique texts and then comparing those texts with Amerindian traditions and practices. Lafitau primarily wanted to persuade his readers of the unity of humanity, especially in the realm of religion. Second, he wanted to demonstrate the importance of understanding Amerindians in order to understand the antique past.

THE RELIGIOUS UNITY OF HUMANITY

One of the most illuminating and yet neglected aspects of Lafitau's thought is his theory of religion.[16] He was adamant all humanity had a religion and that, indeed, humanity's need for religion revealed the universality of religion, a view consistent with that of his fellow Jesuits in the New World.[17] "Men need a religion ... But this necessity for a religion is, at the same time, proof of its existence since its basis is the unanimous belief of all nations which have had, in all times, an object for their veneration and worship."[18]

Lafitau rejected the idea there were any people in the world without religion. He saw religion in two ways. First, Lafitau believed religion was important for the maintenance of society. And second, he believed all religion sprang from the same source: "It is impossible that these nations, so very different in their manner of thinking, which have conceived such

---

15. Northeast, *The Parisian Jesuits*: "Jesuit commentators [in the Journal Trevoux] scarcely differed from Voltaire and the writers of the Enlightenment in their concept of imagination and their general critical assumptions. The marriage of ethical and aesthetic ideals that informed the Jesuit view of literature was the common currency of the 18th century theorists, whether Christian or otherwise; it was a point of contact with secular-minded men of letters, not a source of conflict" (28).

16. Elizabeth L. Moore, one of the translators of *Moeurs*, wrote of Lafitau: "His theoretical religious discussions are so involved and torturous as to be less interesting." Lafitau, *Moeurs*, 81–92. She was not alone in her reaction to Lafitau's writing on religion.

17. Northeast, *The Parisian Jesuits*: "Universal Salvation the only position consistent with Jesuit insistence on divine mercy and human free-will" (160). For Jesuits, universalized Christianity meant that different faiths represent different traditions but all are part of a divine providential plan, and that Christ's sacrifice redeemed all humanity.

18. Lafitau, *Moeurs*, 92.

diverse ideas in the use of things most essential for life, would have been able to agree on this one point, that there is a God, the author of religion as he is its object, had this belief not been *engraved in the hearts of all men at the same time* as it is portrayed outwardly by the beauty of his works."[19] [my emphasis] All religion, Lafitau believed, led back to the Christian God and humanity's original parents—Adam and Eve. All humanity had been created by the same God and, in the moment of creation, given knowledge of religion. Lafitau felt a study of pagan mythology would demonstrate the spiritual unity of humanity. "In this same doctrine [pagan mythology] we see a religion, pure and holy in itself and in its origin, a religion emanating from God who gave it to our first fathers."[20] Believing in unity between Europeans and Amerindians on theological grounds, he was determined to demonstrate that unity through observance and practice of religion. Evidence of the Christian God could be found in pagan mythology, provided one knew how to look for it.

In this Lafitau differed from Acosta, who argued Amerindian religion was given to them by the Devil who mimics God at every turn ("he wants to imitate God and compete with him and his Holy Law").[21] Therefore, Acosta attributed the similarities he found between Christianity and pagan religion to the Devil's mimesis, the diabolical desire to be like God and to have the worship properly due only to God. Lafitau's position, however, was a much more developed form of Jesuit accommodation of Amerindian religion, an attitude primarily indicated by Lafitau's emphasis on the original unity of humanity.[22] For Lafitau the many similarities between "true religion" (i.e. Christianity) and pagan religion could be explained by the observation all religion shared the same source: "There is . . . in this religion of the first pagan peoples, such a great resemblance with several points of belief taught by faith and presupposing a revelation, such conformity in the forms of worship with those of true religion that it seems almost all its essential points have been based on the same foundation [as that of true religion]."[23] By carefully reading pagan myths, searching for similarities in

19. Ibid.

20. Ibid., 34.

21. Acosta, *Historia*, 327. See chapter 2.

22. Acosta felt he had to account for human sacrifice theologically and developed his theory of mimesis as a result. Lafitau was not directly confronted with the practice and, through the luxury of distance, was able to adopt a different type of theory.

23. Lafitau, *Moeurs*, 31–32.

63

story elements within Amerindian mythology, Lafitau believed he could trace the spiritual development of humanity. He wanted to show the ways the "passions . . . which poison the best things" led humanity away from God's initial revelation.[24] In the "confusion and disorder" that result from the passions, humans are separated from God.[25] Yet because of this initial revelation wherein God "engraved" knowledge of true religion "on the hearts of all men," Lafitau included Amerindians and the peoples of antiquity in the Christian world, the Christian faith, and the Christian afterlife. Lafitau argued there were many examples in pagan religion that proved the "conformity" of pagan religion and Christianity: "We find, for example, vestiges of the mystery of the Very Holy Trinity [fn 1] in the mysteries of Isis, in the works of Plato, in the religions of the East and West Indies, Japan and Mexico. As I shall show in the following chapters, we discover several other similar features in pagan mythology."[26] Those similar features were the root of Lafitau's system. Finding vestiges of the trinity, the creation story, and Old Testament practices in those disparate locales were the proofs Lafitau used to demonstrate "true religion"—i.e. Christianity—was at the root of all religion.

The element that makes Lafitau's system different from previous systems, especially those created by antique authors who attempted to explain and categorize religion or antique paganism, was that Lafitau argued his system affirmed the divine origin of religion—he argued his system had "no temptation toward atheism."[27] Lafitau understood atheists to be strict humanists—people who attributed the creation of religion to humanity rather than to God.[28] "I find, finally, a last advantage in [my system]. It is that, by the way in which I explain pagan mythology and symbolic theology, *I trace the source of the symbols to the Divinity, to the origins of our religion*, not, as pagan philosophers did in the last periods of paganism, to an explanation of the physical world. Their explanations might favour impiety and give support to a refined atheism."[29] By implication Lafitau's system favored faith. He also implied that his system gave support to a universal, if

---

24. Ibid., 35.
25. Ibid.
26. Ibid., 32.
27. Ibid., 35–36.
28. Ibid., 34.
29. Ibid., 35–36, emphasis added.

sometimes imperfect, Christianity, though he was careful not to make such a bold claim explicitly.[30]

An example of Lafitau's system will show both his comparative method that found "true religion" at the root of all religion and his distance from Acosta, Las Casas, and Sahagún. Without the kind of missionary-ethnographers preceding him, Lafitau's "system" would not be possible. For example, following Sahagún's advice to missionaries in the sixteenth-century, Lafitau writes "one must never take it upon oneself to describe the manners and customs of a country on which there are no systematic studies unless one knows the language."[31] By the time Lafitau entered the Society of Jesus, knowledge of indigenous languages was mandatory for all Jesuit missionaries. Many missionaries, Lafitau probably included, learned indigenous languages through immersion. Standing on the shoulders of the missionary-ethnographers writing in the sixteenth-century, Lafitau learned the language in order to describe the customs and manners of the Amerindians.

After a few caveats about the limitations of his system and his desire to learn still more from others with greater knowledge, Lafitau launched into his system. He had been hinting at it through a discussion of Iroquois cosmology in a chapter entitled *The Origin of the Peoples of America*. Lafitau accounted for the presence of Amerindians in the Americas through an exploration of biblical texts, antique accounts of various lands, and a form of comparative mythology. Lafitau concluded Amerindians were the "barbarians" of Greek lore, who occupied Greece before the Greeks and then immigrated to the Americas.[32] Lafitau wrote he could "recognize the Iroquois and Huron . . . in those peoples of Asiatic Thrace who, from the extremities of Asia Minor and even of Lycia" traveled across the ancient world.[33] Lafitau could "recognize" these people through comparing stories from both of their religions.

---

30. In his critical introduction to *Moeurs*, Fenton says that Lafitau wrote a "lost treatise" on primitive religion, which "scandalously suggested" there is one universal deity, was denied publication by the French royal censor and all copies are now lost (xxxix). Fenton hints that Lafitau thought his work was blocked by the jealousy of another Jesuit but Fenton gives no citation.

31. Lafitau, *Moeurs*: "It is significant that Lafitau repeatedly stressed the importance of language as a key to the understanding of peoples, although his actual comparisons of words were often erroneous" (94).

32. Ibid., 89.

33. Ibid., 92.

Work Useful to Religion and the Humanities

To fully explicate his comparison and show the similarities between the Greek barbarians and Amerindians, as well as trace their relationship to the Bible, Lafitau examined the following creation story. He attributed this story to the Iroquois, and found it corroborated by tribes in Brazil and Peru as well.[34] In this story, six men were floating in the wind before there was an earth. The six men were concerned they were the last of their people because there were no women. Somehow they learned there was a woman in heaven (Lafitau notes he doesn't know where they learn this) and pointed themselves in that direction. When they arrived at heaven, the six men appointed one of their number, the Wolf, to approach the woman. According to Lafitau, the woman was easily seduced: "[a] curious woman who likes to talk and receive presents does not delay long in yielding. This one was weak even in heaven itself."[35] Because of her "weakness," the king of heaven was enraged and evicted the woman and her new companion from heaven. The woman fell from heaven and landed on a turtle, who, with the help of otters and fishes, dug up enough clay to create land masses. The woman and the man had two children, both males. These male children fought and because one of the boys possessed superior weapons he was able to kill the other one. The evidence of the woman's "weakness" and the death of one of their sons at the hands of another showed this woman and man to be the mother and father of all humanity: "All other men have their descent from this woman through a long succession of generations, and it is such a singular event as this which has served, they say, as a basis for the division of the three families of the Iroquois and Hurons, into those of the Wolf, the Bear and the Turtle which, by their very names, are a living tradition bringing before their eyes the history of the first times."[36] This story, Lafitau argued, was the biblical story of the garden of Eden that had been distorted and confused by the passage of time and geographical drift. Nonetheless, it was the account from Genesis chapter three. Lafitau argued the story revealed: "[the] tree of knowledge of good and evil, the temptation into which she [Eve] had the misfortune to fall, which some heretics have believed to be the sin of the flesh [a belief] founded, perhaps, on an alteration by pagan ideas; we discover in it [the story] the wrath of God driving out our first ancestors from the place of delights where he had placed them . . .; finally

---

34. Ibid., 81–84.
35. Ibid., 84.
36. Ibid., 82.

we think that we can see the murder of Abel killed by his brother, Cain."[37] Through this story, the God of revelation gave the vision of the true origin of humanity to the Amerindians before they could have the knowledge of the true version through the Bible. In his analysis, Lafitau added this particular story also reveals the root of a common heresy—that sex was the cause of the fall from grace that left all humans in a depraved state, incapable of good works. Jesuits of the time maintained Adam's sin was a stain and that he was deprived of his "supernatural gifts as a result of the fall" but Adam's capacity for moral action remained intact after the fall and as a result all humans were capable of good works and participating in the process of salvation through grace.[38]

This kind of mythic comparison was only the first step of Lafitau's system. With it he established the connection between the Amerindians and the Biblical account of the origin of humanity. For the next step, connecting Amerindians to the ancients, Lafitau turned from Amerindian mythology to Homer. Lafitau compared above Amerindian story to Homer's account of Até's expulsion from Olympus.[39] Lafitau saw this story as another version of the story of Eve cast from paradise. "Homer's story of Até's fall is an exact prototype of the Iroquois fable of the woman driven from heaven."[40] Because Homer offered a prototype of the expulsion story, Lafitau argued the story must have some connection to the story of the expulsion of humanity's first parents from the garden of Eden. Homer preserved this kernel of true religion which was visible to Lafitau's discerning eye despite the differences from the account in Genesis. This demonstrates Lafitau's belief in human unity across time (before Christ) and across culture (non-European, non-Christian).

---

37. Ibid., 81–84.
38. Northeast, *The Parisian Jesuits*, 156.
39. Homer, *Iliad* 19.85.
40. Lafitau, *Moeurs*, 83–85. In order to make this argument, Lafitau addressed Justin Martyr's interpretation of Homer's story of Até's fall in his *Exhortation to the Greeks*. Justin argues Homer's story represents the rebellion of the angels and their expulsion from heaven. In the Iliad, Até's spends her life wrecking havoc on humanity. Justin interprets this as the angels' jealousy of humanity's salvation and their goal to put as many obstacles as possible between humanity and grace. Lafitau argued that Homer portrays Até as a woman and because of that, she's not an angel but actually a woman. Lafitau cursorily investigates her name and its roots and claims, "Até may also be the name given Eve by which she was called in the feasts for the barbarians from whom Homer took this fable" (84).

Work Useful to Religion and the Humanities

Lafitau highlighted significant elements in the Iroquois story that connected it to other stories throughout the world. For example, Lafitau emphasized the presence of the turtle who caught the woman. Lafitau traced the image of the turtle through Harpocrates, the Greek form of the Egyptian God Horus. In "ancient monuments" Harpocrates has turtles at his feet.[41] Lafitau continued the historical comparison, noting the Goddess Venus Urania "was the author of the harmony of the world, portrayed by the turtle, the symbol of this harmony."[42] Lastly, Lafitau turned to the far east to bring in another connection religion to his comparative model: "[i]n the East Indian religion the Brahmans have a tradition of their God Vishnu metamorphosed into a turtle."[43] Through this similar element—the presence of the turtle—all the religious traditions of the world were connected to their original source, the biblical account of creation. Lafitau argued this connection could be clearly seen through these consistent elements. These components demonstrated the connection between the pagan myths and pointed to their origin in the Christian tradition. Lafitau demonstrated the religious unity of humanity over space and time by connecting these elements to the biblical narrative.

The presence of the turtle in all these traditions led Lafitau to two conclusions. First, the Iroquois were descendents of the "barbarians" described in Homer and "the Greeks may well have *borrowed from them* the plot of this [Até's fall] story"[44] [my emphasis]. Second, "[t]he fact that the background of this fable is everywhere the same proves that the turtle is the symbol of that ancient religion . . ."[45] In other words, the Amerindians are direct descendents of the ancient peoples of the Mediterranean and are directly connected to European life and the God of revelation. Lafitau argued he could see the ways these myths were connected through the similarities of the stories and the presence of the turtle in all three. These stories and the threads of connection that seem to wind around the globe are Lafitau's proof of divine providence and religious unity.

---

41. Ibid., 84.

42. This is from an translation of *Oedipus Aegytoacis* by brother Jesuit Athanasius Kircher; ibid., 85.

43. Ibid., 86.

44. Ibid., 85, emphasis added. It is notable that Lafitau attributes the borrowing of elements to the Greeks rather than to the Amerindians.

45. Ibid.

Proofs of religion were not only found in religious stories and myths but also in the practice of religion. Sacrifice, Lafitau wrote, "is an act of religion, an offering made to the divinity" out of obligation and especially in "gratitude for the benefits" humans receive from God.[46] Sacrifice was as old as religion itself and was "customary" in all religions. Because of this customary practice, Lafitau argued sacrifice itself was a proof of religion.

Sacrifice had important common elements across the various human nations and cultures. Sacrificing either domesticated animals or, in places where there were no domesticated animals, sacrificing animals "taken in hunting" was a regular practice.[47] As people became more wealthy and had greater resources at their disposal, their sacrifices became more magnificent. However, no matter the relative wealth of a given people "whatever their conditions, they sacrificed always their most highly prized possessions."[48]

On the question of the Mexicans and their sacrifices that had so troubled his missionary-ethnographer predecessors, Lafitau was subdued. He made very little reference to Mexico and the practice of human sacrifice even in the section of his book devoted to the practice of sacrifice. Just has he had little to say about the "demon," Lafitau made only one mention of the practice of human sacrifice in Mexico.[49] He reported the "Mexicans offered many human victims as sacrifices."[50] And, rather than exploring the nature and practice of this sacrifice, Lafitau moved immediately to generalizations about "other primitive peoples." He wrote such sacrifices "were not so usual nor so marked unless we regard as a sacrifice the punishments which they made their captives or prisoners of war undergo. I think this

46. Ibid., 132.

47. Ibid., 133.

48. Ibid.

49. "It was only towards the end of the fifteenth century that these immense regions were discovered by one of those events seemingly born of change but really reserved by God in the treasures of his Providence for the happy moment marked by the grace of the Redeemer to enlighten, with the light of faith, the *innumerable nations held in slavery by the demon*, buried in the darkness of error, in the shades of death and plunged in all the horrors always resulting from brutal ferocity and the errors of idolatry" (ibid., 42, [my emphasis]). This quote is an isolated reference to the Devil in *Moeurs* and acknowledgement of the interpretation given to pagan religions by missionary-ethnographers prior to Lafitau. However, Lafitau does not return to this theme of Amerindians as the slaves of the Devil. Instead he focuses on tracing the elements of pagan myths back to antiquity and the Bible with no starring or supporting role for the devil.

50. Ibid., 133.

rather probable."⁵¹ There are two significant points here. First, human sacrifices were "not so usual." And second, human sacrifice was in line with sacrifices made by tribes who had sacrificed their prisoners of war. Lafitau put human sacrifice in line with other practices of sacrifice, especially those peoples who sacrificed their most prized and magnificent things.

In that sole paragraph on human sacrifice, Lafitau said in the "ancient Relations of North America," there is only one other kind of sacrifice connected to the Old Testament. That was the "sacrifice like that offered by the Canaanites to Moloch."[52] Lafitau was referring here to the sacrifice of the first born child. This sacrifice is committed by the "king of the tribe" and if Lafitau was aware of the Amerindian reasoning behind this sacrifice, he did not write about it.[53] It is the identical example Acosta used in his discussion of the same issue.[54]

Just as he argues sacrifice was universal, Lafitau argued belief in the existence of the soul was a universal belief found across time and throughout all human societies: "[A]t all times, there has been recognized in man a soul quite distinct from his body, a soul which was a substance extremely subtile [sic] and fine" and eternal.[55] Lafitau believed souls were "an emmanation [sic] or a portion even of the divinity" which united the whole of humanity. Within the soul was "contained the principle of life, of one's thoughts, wishes, and all one's deeds . . ." the sum of all the parts of what was essential about humanity. This common human belief in the soul was enhanced by the further belief the "body could perish without its [the soul] perishing as a consequence, and [it is the soul] which survives the dust of the tomb."[56] Belief in the eternal life of the soul pervaded Amerindian life and Amerindians attributed the same qualities of the soul to humans and animals.

Lafitau noted Amerindians believed animals "possess a great deal of reason and intelligence.[57] As seen with the turtle in the creation story

---

51. Ibid.

52. Ibid.

53. Ibid. Lafitau doesn't say whether it is the first born child of every couple or every village; in fact, for such a detail oriented writer, this section is lamentably under researched.

54. See chapter 2.

55. Lafitau, *Moeurs*, 229–30.

56. Ibid.

57. Ibid., 230.

above, Lafitau believed animals and animal totems played an important role in Amerindian religion. Lafitau wrote Amerindians believe they speak the language of animals. Even more importantly, Lafitau told his readers, Amerindians "think that beasts survive their body" just as human spirits do. Further, Lafitau added Amerindians believed each animal species has a perfect form. While the Amerindians are unclear on the actual location, they believed there is a "country of souls" where "the type and model of all others contained in this [any given] species" resided.[58] Lafitau concluded from this belief that Amerindians had made "a return to Plato's beliefs."[59] For Lafitau this was a profound connection, giving greater credence to his system. If Amerindians knew of the pleroma, even in the realm of their imaginations, the implication was Lafitau's theory of a direct connection between Amerindians and ancients was even more strongly supported.[60]

However, it was not, for Lafitau, necessarily a "correct" belief, regardless of the close connection to Plato. Lafitau had said he would not ruminate on the relative errors of Amerindian beliefs but he did attempt to account for how error might have occurred beyond the role of human imagination.[61] It was through "a sequel of errors of paganism and the corruption of religion that our Indians, in imitation of the ancients, have given spirituality to the souls of beasts and attributed to them a kind of immortality like that which they attribute to their own [souls]."[62] The role of imitation is very important here. It supported Lafitau's argument Amerindians were direct descendents of the "ancients" and pointed to a mutual corruption. The Amerindians were "imitating" the error of the ancients. Both Amerindians and the ancients shared this error in religious thought.

58. Ibid.

59. Ibid.

60. Lafitau excuses himself from commenting on the relative truth or error of beliefs about the soul and then expounds on the connection between Amerindian beliefs about the soul and what Plato taught. "The idea of the spirit as being above the sense and the senses nevertheless having always played the important part in men's manner of thinking, would be difficult to retain in its pure state and not to find it greatly altered by the imagination so that the spirit might have come to be represented under palpable images, subject to corporeality, divisibility and other properties of matter" (229). Errors in belief can be attributed to human imagination, which plays a powerful role in the development and diffusion of Christian ideas throughout the Amerindian world. Without the guiding principle of the church and tradition human imagination will construct solutions, some of which are not far from the beliefs of the ancients. Ibid., 229.

61. Ibid.

62. Ibid., 231.

Lafitau concluded even though the Amerindians have this belief in animal souls, they "accord mankind... a great superiority over all other animals."[63] There was a kernel of truth in Amerindian belief—humans were superior to all other creatures—even though there was the "error" of belief with regard to eternal souls and animals.

Through these elements and similarities in belief and practice, Lafitau argued the Amerindians and the ancients had received the core of true religion before the advent of Christianity in their world. He also argued these similarities demonstrated the genealogy of the Amerindians, showing their relation to the barbarians of antiquity. Having demonstrated these two key points, Lafitau used his system of comparison to look at ancient practices in Amerindian life.

THE PRACTICES OF BURIAL AND ATHENROSERA

In addition to being able to use antique culture and authors to demonstrate the religious unity of humanity, Lafitau used Amerindian culture and practices to understand aspects of antique culture. He developed an understanding of Amerindian culture as a window on the antique past. In this section, I will show how Lafitau's understanding of antique culture is further developed through surviving examples of antique practices found in Amerindian culture.

Lafitau devoted an entire chapter of *Moeurs* to the study of burial practices across New World traditions and through antique authors. This is another example of Lafitau's system of understanding Amerindian religion in relation to antique sources. Lafitau used Amerindians' practices to shed light on accounts from antique authors and show examples of practices reported in antique texts.

Lafitau enumerated four types of burial practices: burial, burning, sacrifice, and corpse abuse (dead consumed by carrion eaters). The first, and most ancient Lafitau adds, is by "inhumation" or burial.[64] This practice was used by the "Patriarchs of the Old Testament," the Egyptians and the Persians. The other practices were introduced through "superstition, caprice, fear of profanation and other passions."[65] Lafitau does not clarify what exactly those fears and superstitions are led the ancients away from

63. Ibid.
64. Ibid., 224.
65. Ibid.

the practice of burial, but burial was the appropriate method and all other methods were "errors." After burial, fire was the next most ancient method of burying the dead. The remains were placed in an urn. This practice, from India and ancient Greece, found its opposite in Persia. The ancient Persians thought that fire was a divinity and to burn a body in that divine fire was a great profanity. Lafitau briefly discussed nations that are not "permitted to bury their dead before exposing them to the dogs and vultures" and from the "way that these animals went about devouring them" drew conclusions as to their "happy or unhappy state" in eternity.[66]

This led Lafitau to a discussion of peoples who abused the corpses of their dead. First of the "other more barbarous nations" were the people of India and Scythia who sacrificed their parents "when they come to a certain age . . . to make a feast for their friends."[67] Still other ancient peoples exposed their sick in the forests, who were then devoured by beasts "forestalling hunger and other sufferings by such a cruel abandonment."[68] There were people from "Colchis" who buried their women and hung the bodies of men, sewn into ox skins, from trees.[69]

After compiling this list, Lafitau offered the analysis the antique authors "who have spoken of these customs have, perhaps, told the truth if we consider the heart and substance of things, I believe, nevertheless, that most of them are partly false in respect to certain details which represent these peoples to us as much more barbarous than they actually were."[70] Lafitau was confident these antique authors were exaggerating these customs because he saw in America "many similar ones [customs] are practiced" and through careful examination Lafitau thought he could "uncover motives which soften . . . and correct, characteristics which these practices, regarded in themselves alone, present at first as too barbarous."[71] He granted it was true some tribes "put their old men to death" but he said those tribes do that as a "service in delivering them from the discomforts of an old age which conditions make more disagreeable than death itself."[72] In other words, the

66. Ibid., 225.
67. Ibid.
68. Ibid.
69. Ibid.
70. Ibid., 225–26.
71. Ibid., 226.
72. Ibid.

action was motivated by reason, sparing the elderly of the discomforts of old age, rather than barbarism.

Lafitau conceded there are people who ate their relatives but they "do so only through piety, misled piety certainly, but still *piety coloured with some shade of reason*, for they think that they are giving them a burial much more honourable than if they abandoned them to the worms and the dust."[73] [my emphasis] It is this "shade of reason" Lafitau argued the Amerindians were bringing to the ancient accounts. These practices, once thought to be barbarous and irrational, now could be observed. Through observation, Lafitau concluded these practices had reason. It was reason not readily apparent in the antique accounts but reason was intelligible through the observation of Amerindian practices. Lafitau argued it "may be also that the ancient authors were mistaken" in their statements about the Thracians' joy at death and grief at birth, for example. Lafitau argued the ancient authors may have been "led into error" by not understanding that the ancient Thracians danced and sang because "in their concept and their language, [to dance and sing are] the same thing as to weep."[74] He believed this was a possible explanation, because South American Amerindian practices were similar and were motivated by grief expressed through singing.

As for people who ate the flesh of their relatives, Lafitau found this practice, too, in South America. He reported this was practiced on the warriors of the culture (Lafitau did not indicate how the warriors died, whether by war or natural causes). The corpses were then "respectfully" conserved for some time until finally the skeletons were carried "into battle in the guise of standards, to renew their [the living warriors] courage by the sight of them and inspire terror in their enemies."[75] Lafitau used these Amerindian practices to shed light on seemingly barbaric or incomprehensible reports from antique authors.

Lafitau found the Huron perform the same rites for their dead that "Nicholas of Damascus said that the Phrygians used to do for corpses of their priests" by leaving the bodies of the dead on elevated platforms.[76] Amerindians "even sometimes observe what Herodotus recounts of the Nasamons"[77] who bury people in the "same position as an embryo in the

73. Ibid.
74. Ibid.
75. Ibid.
76. Ibid., 227.
77. Ibid.

maternal womb."[78] These examples exhibited the power of Lafitau's system. He was not only able to demonstrate the veracity of at least some of the antique accounts but he was also able to temper some of the more "barbaric" accounts with more information and context from antiquity. He demonstrated how, through the help of Amerindian examples, antique practices appeared barbaric were really pious actions grounded in reason and was thereby able to show the presence of piety tempered with reason in both antique and Amerindian religion.

Lafitau also used this section on burial to rebuke some European Christian practices. Examples of this kind of rebuke are rare in Lafitau's text but they highlight his initial point "[p]eople should study customs only in order to form customs. Everywhere there is something from which we can profit."[79] Amerindians "look upon death more tranquilly than we [Europeans] do."[80] Because of this tranquil outlook Amerindians were "not troubled with a false compassion and the delicacy shameful to Christians which makes people dare not announce to a dying man the danger in which he is, although it is a question of his eternity which they would rather risk than frighten him."[81] Instead, Lafitau opined, perhaps the Amerindians had a better system for dealing with impending death. "It happens often enough among these barbarians that a sick man is told that it is all over, that he can no longer live."[82] After this declaration the Amerindians offered "precious robes and ornaments" to the dying person. There was sometimes a farewell feast for the dying person. These tokens of esteem and affection were presented with the "same zeal and principle of tenderness as made Penelope work with so much care on the burial robes of her father-in-law, Laertes."[83] The dying person (man, in this example) was composed and organized himself as though he were preparing for a voyage. Lafitau ended this digression with the question "How many Europeans at this fatal moment would die with horror at such a preparation?"[84]

Lafitau focused on the practice of burying "precious furnishing, great wealth" and other offerings in tombs or on funeral pyres, corroborating

78. Ibid.
79. Ibid., 28.
80. Ibid., 227.
81. Ibid.
82. Ibid.
83. Ibid.
84. Ibid.

this Amerindian practice to a discussion of the Gauls from Caesar's *Commentaries*.[85] Certain "brave Gauls" were pledged to a "great man" and the result was "if it should happen that he perished, they all put themselves to death with him, or committed suicide after his defeat . . .."[86] There was not a single person "within the memory of man" who did not honor this practice if he or she were so pledged.[87] Lafitau found this practice among the chief and the "chieftainess" of the Natchez in Louisiana. These "devoted ones" accompanied the chief or chieftainess everywhere, ate at their expense and "share[d] in all their honours and misfortunes."[88] The greatest of all the "misfortunes" was the death of the man or woman to whom their life was wholly pledged. When that chief or chieftainess died, these people were put to death at the burial ceremony. Through "established custom" the "devoted ones" were strangled and died "ceremoniously."[89] This was not the only example: Lafitau also found an account by Lopez de Gomara regarding "the Spanish Island" demonstrated another example of this practice.[90] These practices, which involved killing devoted persons, slaves, and wives, were at least modified if not completely stopped by the presence of European missionaries.[91]

Lafitau concluded "no idea is more marked among the Indians in general than respect for the dead and for the memory of their ancestors."[92] This was so true that among Amerindians, even those that live in very cold climes, the best furs, textiles, and woolen robes were "destined for funeral duties."[93] This practice "impoverishes them [the living] almost completely."[94] These presents were displayed in the home of the deceased, on poles, at the pyres, in the lodge and in the cemetery depending on the tribe in question.[95] There was a "notable" who "makes a distribution of

85. Ibid., 228.
86. Ibid.
87. Ibid.
88. Ibid., 229.
89. Ibid.
90. Fenton and Moore provide this reference. Lopez de Gomara, *Histoire Génerale des Indies*, Book 1, Chapter 28. Ibid.
91. Ibid., 229.
92. Ibid., 230.
93. Ibid.
94. Ibid.
95. There are six tribes of the Iroquois with varying practices. While Lafitau is often vague about his informants, he did display detailed knowledge of the Iroquois and

these pious legacies."⁹⁶ The ultimate value of these gifts and offerings could be very great, depending on "the position and rank" of the deceased."⁹⁷ These distributions also had an ancient precedent. Similar practices "were common among the Romans. They consisted of money and other things [held] in common use like wheat, wine, oil, meats, salt. This custom is still apparent on medals, inscriptions, epitaphs and all the other monuments remaining from the debris of antiquity."⁹⁸ Lafitau connected the practices of Amerindians as closely to those of ancient Europeans as he could. He drew on antique texts, both literary and historical, to connect to living Amerindian practices. Where he could, he used Amerindian practices to modify and clarify antique accounts. Lastly, in very few instances, Lafitau presented Amerindian practices to admonish European Christians for their less-than-Christian behavior.

The strongest example of how Lafitau's method showed the lives of the ancients in living color in the New World is *athenrosera*, or "warrior pairs." Lafitau chose the example of *athenrosera* because he saw it as one "of the most interesting points" of Amerindian culture and because that relationship provided one of "the most curious comparisons with antiquity."⁹⁹ He compared Amerindian warrior pairs with famous warrior pairs from antique history. He argued the Amerindian practices "explain to us the usage, particularly in Cretan and Spartan Republics," of the role of the warrior pair in society.¹⁰⁰

Lafitau told his readers how the legislators of the Cretan and Spartan republics had been "slandered" by statements that implied the relationship of the *Amator* and *Amasius* was something dishonorable. However, Lafitau stated it was unlikely such "wise lawgivers" would have authorized anything that would make their republics "eternally infamous." Additionally, Lafitau defended, if "that most abominable of the vices and the one most offensive to reason had been attached to friendships of this sort, the lawgivers would not have been careful to honor them to such a point that the men most sought after, accepted it as a merit and a sign of honor . . ."¹⁰¹ In other

---

Huron. See Daniel K. Richter, *The Ordeal of the Longhouse*.
96. Lafitau, *Moeurs*, 230.
97. Ibid.
98. Ibid., 230–31.
99. Ibid., 362.
100. Ibid.
101. Ibid.

words, while the devotion of the warrior partners could not be questioned neither was the devotion of the warrior partners defiled by "infamous acts," i.e., homosexuality.

In order for the ancients to ensure the *athenrosera* relationship was not sexual in nature, Lafitau pointed to the Platonic ideal of male friendship as the root of these relationships across cultures. According to Lafitau the point of the lover/beloved friendship established "relationships which had virtue as their principle, which were decent connections, innocent friendships, a meetings of minds, from which even the shadow of crime was lacking, and which were a reciprocal emulation of the one loving and the one loved as Plato defined it in several places."[102] Lafitau further explained this relationship from antiquity. The lawmakers held the lover responsible for the beloved, who was considered a sort of disciple of the lover. The lover was bound to guarantee the conduct of the beloved and should the beloved transgress it was the lover who would pay the penalty. Same-sex relations were a heresy and a crime and in Lafitau's church the doctrine against same-sex relationships had been a staple of church controversy since Paul.[103] Lafitau reinforced a Platonic understanding of friendship and gently refuted similar charges of infamy made against the Society of Jesus.[104]

Continuing to assure his readers of the purity of these lover-beloved relationships in antiquity, Lafitau quoted Claudius Aelianus, saying if the beloved "happened to conceive criminal desires for the object of his affection, there was no safety for him in Sparta . . ."[105] The beloved could only be saved by fleeing the country in shame.[106] However, Lafitau was certain this "criminal desire" is not the fault of the "lawgivers" who established and defended the "particular friendships" because "vice slips in everywhere and there is nothing free from abuse."[107] Lafitau acknowledged these relationships were deeply important in antiquity: "[I]f we pay attention to the history of the first times, we shall see that almost all the heroes were thus united to some friend who was the companion of their travails and

102. Ibid.

103. Boswell, *Christianity, Social Tolerance, and Homosexuality*. And is still a source of controversy today.

104. Andre Rivet, *The State-Mysteries of the Iesuites*.

105. Aelian, *Varia Historia*. Claudius Aelianus (c. AD 175—c. 235). "Varia Historia," originally written in Greek in the third century AD, contains a miscellany of anecdotes, lists, biographical sketches and descriptions of natural wonders.

106. Lafitau, *Moeurs*, 263.

107. Ibid., 363.

The Comparative Method and Reflections of Antiquity

their good fortune. Such were Hercules and Iolaus, ... Achilles and Patrocles, ... Orestes and Pylades."[108] Lafitau struggled with the accusations raised against these intense male/male relationships and came to the conclusion, while nothing human can be totally free from vice and sin, it was possible for men to have the kind of idealized friendship so valued by Plato. More important, these idealized relationships were alive and well in the New World, demonstrating a direct connection from Amerindians to Plato.

Lafitau reported on these "particular friendships" in the New World, though he gave far less information about Amerindians than he did about antique society. From various accounts in the Jesuit Relations and Jean de Léry's *Histoire du Brésil*, Lafitau gleaned as much information as he could regarding the structure and practice of these "particular" friendships.[109] Lafitau learned such relationships were also called "the perfect ally" and those alliances were so strong that all their goods and property were held in common, "as if they were a single person."[110]

Among the North American Amerindians, Lafitau reported these particular friendships carried no suspicion of apparent vice. However Lafitau worried "there is or may be much real vice."[111] These relationships were very ancient in origin and sacred "in the union they form, the knots of which are as closely tied as those of blood and nature . . ."[112] These strong ties could only be broken if one of the friends made himself unworthy through cowardice and thereby dishonored himself, his friend, and their relationship. Lafitau reported Amerindian parents encouraged these friendships among their children and respected their rights. These friendships were built through gifts made by the friend to his selected friend; they were maintained by mutual marks of affection; the two became constant companions "in hunting, warfare, and good or bad fortune; they are entitled to food and shelter in each other's lodging . . . Finally, these friendships grow old with them and are so well cemented that often there is heroism in them as there is between Orestes and Pylades."[113] Also in the *Jesuit Relations*, Lafitau

---

108. Ibid., 364. "Plutarch in the life of Pelops, tells us that these pairs of friends sent offerings to the tomb of Iolaus in memory of his friendship with Hercules and bound together the knots of their alliance by the vows made in his name, invoking him."

109. Ibid., 363–65.

110. Ibid., 364. Jean de Lery, *History of a Voyage*.

111. Lafitau, *Moeurs*, 364.

112. Ibid.

113. Ibid.

found an account by one priest, who reported that if one of the friends was killed ceremonially or by torture the other would seek the same fate, and usually, find it.[114]

Lafitau ended some chapters with his final opinion, usually demonstrating how he differed from other New World chroniclers or interpreters of antique culture about the reading they have given to Amerindian practices. Lafitau ended this chapter with a story from the *Jesuit Relations* of two "particular friends," one of whom was sentenced to be burned to death. The other friend was so distraught that he demanded and was granted the same fate. Prior to the burning, both were baptized by their village missionary and they "died in a great sentiment of piety."[115] In the final paragraph of this chapter Lafitau wrote of an occurrence in a Jesuit mission he knew of—he does not indicate which one—where the missionaries suppressed these particular friendships because of the vices they feared from them. However missionaries did not tell the Amerindians why they were suppressing the friendships. Regardless the Amerindians were "not at all angry about it because these friendships were too costly and became, for that reason, too burdensome."[116]

For Lafitau, these relationships from antiquity were problematic for a number of reasons. "Warrior pairs" were accused of the most "infamous" abuses and were subjected to strong attacks and equally strong defenses. Yet, for all intents and purposes, "warrior pairs" were not part of Lafitau's own eighteenth-century European world. Lafitau found in the suppression of these friendships in the New World an explanation for their demise in antiquity—they were costly and burdensome to the community. The relationships were also fraught with peril and the closeness of the friendship combined the threat of infamy along with the threat of dual loss for the community. If one of the "particular friends" was lost through capture or death, generally the other would meet the same fate. These relationships were also sought after and greatly admired: the friends had the support and adoration of the community and were subject to special circumstances and privileges. For all these reasons then "particular friendships" were therefore burdensome and costly to the Amerindians as well as the ancients.

This example of Lafitau's comparative system illuminates his understanding of "warrior pairs" and his vision of both Amerindians and antique

114. Ibid., 364–65. He admits this is a word of mouth report.
115. Ibid., 365.
116. Ibid.

The Comparative Method and Reflections of Antiquity

texts. Lafitau viewed the Amerindians through the lens of Greek and Roman authors, and this lens in turn functioned as a window that allowed Lafitau to see the Greco-Roman past come alive. Looking through the window at the ancients, Lafitau connected Amerindians with Europeans and to the European past. Looking back through the window at the Amerindians likewise provided Lafitau a way to explain the antique past and see it in action.[117] This is the truly innovative aspect of Lafitau's thought. He used Amerindian culture to give himself and his readership a new view of the past, through the looking glass, as it were for Lafitau. It is as if the entire history of the world was now open to view through multiple, shifting perspectives. The New World provided a way to see the past; the past provided a way to see the New World.

CONCLUSION

Lafitau's theory of religion had only one simple thesis: all religion, ancient or Amerindian, sprang from the same source, the God of revelation. Lafitau's complex theology was a cross-cultural (Amerindians, Indians, Chinese) and cross-temporal (Greeks, Egyptians) theology of divine providence and grace. "I have . . . said enough to show that the Author of Nature has not so hidden himself from these tribes that he has permitted whole nations to remain in ignorance of him . . ."[118] Lafitau argued God would not create any creature without having planted the seed of knowledge of true religion in that creature. Having established the unity of humanity, Lafitau could then use seemingly "pagan" practices and beliefs for the greater edification of Christians. He did this by looking for the practices and beliefs of antiquity in the living world of the Amerindians.

It is this lens-to-window approach demonstrates Lafitau's unique contribution to the history of anthropology. In this chapter I have argued Lafitau developed a particular method of comparison. Without the missionary-ethnographers who wrote before Lafitau, Lafitau's system would not be possible. Lafitau brought a new component to the practice of comparison by using Amerindians to clarify issues about antiquity. Las Casas, Sahagún and Acosta all compared Amerindians with Europeans. Lafitau compared Amerindians with Europeans but he also looked at antiquity and saw it in Amerindians. It is this vision that makes him stand out from

---

117. Pagden, *European Encounters*.
118. Lafitau, *Moeurs*, 281.

Work Useful to Religion and the Humanities

Sahagún and Acosta and stand up as an example for anthropologists and religionists from Tylor to Chidester.

4

The Comparative Method, Religion, and Civilization

He even rationally interprets in this way a custom which to us seems fantastic...

EDWARD BURNETT TYLOR
American Aspects of Anthropology

JOSEPH LAFITAU WAS THE last of a breed. Shortly after his death the Society of Jesus was suppressed and Jesuits were martyred the world over. While the sun had set on the other European empires, it was shining brightly on the British empire, which by the nineteenth century was dominating the intellectual world as well as the economic world. Edward Burnett Tylor represents one of the crowning intellectual glories of British colonialism. Considered the founder of the comparative method as well as of the discipline of anthropology, Tylor put in motion intellectual practices that would dominate the social sciences for years after his death in 1917.[1]

Tylor sought rationality in everything—from the growth of plants and animals to the "laws" of human thought and action. He argued that the

---

1. See Hammel, "The Comparative Method," 145–55. "Although comparison has been used as a technique by earlier writers, The Comparative Method was born in 1889, in a paper by Edward Burnett Tylor delivered to the Royal Anthropological Institute" (146). See also Marett, *Tylor*.

history of humanity was part of the history of nature and as such subject to the same scientific understanding as that of the natural world. R. R. Marett in his biography of Tylor saw this drive toward rationality grounded in Tylor's Quaker heritage.[2] Regardless of the root of his quest to see rational progression in everything Tylor argued that human culture was subject to the same rules as any organic process.

The central thesis of this chapter, that Lafitau and Tylor constructed similar comparative models, has been noted by Margaret Hodgen.[3] However, while she points to this similarity the design of that comparative model has not been thoroughly explored. In this chapter I will explore the similarities and differences between Lafitau and Tylor's comparative models. In the first section of this chapter, I argue that Tylor and Lafitau constructed a similar system for the comparison of human soceieties, particularly in relation to religion. Both were interested in comparison and were looking for ways to understand the development of "religion." Lafitau was a proponent of monogenesis and argued that Christianity and all religions of the world shared the same source: the biblical God of Genesis. Tylor was a cultural progressionist but the root of his system was also singular. While clearly opposed to the degenerationist movement of same period, Tylor was a monogenesist; he argued for a single point of origin for religion found in Natural Religion. Tylor was looking for evidence that all religion developed and evolved along similar lines from a single orginary point. Lafitau would not have used Tylor's scientific language but he would have been sympathetic to Tylor's conclusions about the root of religion (though he would have heartily disapproved of Tylor's Protestantism). And while Tylor might not use much of the language that I will employ here, I trust he would have been sympathetic to my comparative project as well.

In the second part of this chapter, I show how Tylor incorporated various missionary-ethnographer texts in order to use their material for his own system. This is often what scholars do. However, what is important about Tylor's appropriation of missionary texts was his disregard for the Roman Catholic tradition in his understanding of Christianity and the role Roman Catholic tradition played in his reading of the missionaries' texts. Tylor understood Roman Catholics to be less "evolved" in the development of religion from its primitive beginning to its zenith. On the one hand, he

---

2. Marett, *Tylor*.

3. See Hodgen, *Early Anthropology*. It was also hinted at though not developed in Kaspar Kälin's dissertation; see Kälin, *Indianer*.

used missionary-ethnographer texts and other missionary accounts almost as field notes. On the other hand, he discredited missionaries in general and was particularly disdainful toward Catholics. He gave Lafitau high praise—especially for a missionary—but he did not acknowledge his debt to Lafitau's system of comparison.

Tylor was well acquainted with Lafitau's text. He gave Lafitau credit for rationally interpreting the role of the mother's brother in Iroquois society.[4] He commended Lafitau for being a proto-anthropologist. In an 1896 article where Tylor argued for a connection between Asia and North America through "survivals"[5] found in lot-games, Tylor referred to Lafitau as a "missionary-anthropologist."[6] However, despite this admiration, Tylor did not recognize or acknowledge Lafitau's system of comparison.

In this chapter I will explore similarities and differences in the comparative systems that Lafitau and Tylor develop, sites where Lafitau and Tylor shared structures, sources and, to a certain extent, conclusions. I then go on to demonstrate Tylor's approach to Roman Catholic missionaries and the way he categorized Roman Catholic Christianity in his evolutionary understanding of religion. Tylor argued that through the comparison of religious beliefs and practices from diverse cultures he could trace survivals that demonstrated the connections between different stages of religious evolution. Tylor argued his method demonstrated those connections 'organically' as opposed to the Catholic missionaries who, he argued, imposed a sense of unity upon the religious beliefs and practices they found in indigenous cultures.

LAFITAU AND TYLOR FIND MAGIC IN COMPARISON[7]

The similarity between Tylor's and Lafitau's comparative models is explained by their mutual interest in using Amerindians to see previous stages of human religious development and cultural expressions of religious ideas. In this way their questions were very similar: what can Amerindian ("primitives" from Tylor's perspective) beliefs and practices tell about

---

4. Tylor, "American Aspects of Anthropology," 229.

5. See further discussion of the concept of "survivals" below.

6. Tylor, "On American Lot-Games," 55–67. "This learned observant missionary-anthropologist noticed that the American game resembles one brought by the negroes from Africa to the West India Islands."

7. Smith, *Imagining Religion*, 19–35.

Europeans and the origin of religion? Both Tylor and Lafitau were driven to look for the European past in the practices and beliefs of Amerindians; both were looking for the origin of religion. For Lafitau the importance of studying non-Christian cultures and what he called "savage" religion was to see classical history come alive. For Tylor the purpose for comparing what he called "primitive religion" was to see evolution, to trace the history of the development of religion through survivals from animism to deistic Protestantism. Tylor and Lafitau used a similar method and models to construct their theories of the development and growth of religion. Both looked to classical texts and to other missionary documents, particularly those written by missionary-ethnographers such as Las Casas, Sahagún, and Acosta. Tylor's method was enhanced by the use of the folk-lore studies of the Brothers Grimm and by David Hume's *Natural Religion*, sources not available to Lafitau. Both Lafitau and Tylor employed comparative schemas that used "primitive" people (savages) to "see" the human past. This understanding of "primitive religion" gave Lafitau and Tylor the foundation for their respective theories of the single point of origin and the development of human religion.

There is another significant element at play in Tylor's theory of religion: cultural degeneration. The nineteenth-century debate about the origins of "savages"—especially the indigenous peoples of the Americas and Oceania—followed two separate streams, cultural degeneration and cultural evolution.[8] The first stream, cultural degeneration, argued that indigenous and other non-European peoples were remnants of nations that were at one time more civilized. Through war, disease, and natural and biblical disaster, cultural degenerationists argued, indigenous peoples had lost civilization and were therefore at a more primitive stage than westerners.[9] Cultural degenerationists believed that humanity had been created at a relatively civilized state. In other words, for cultural degenerationists, primitive culture did not "evolve" so much as devolve from an original state of civilization. Those peoples who were perceived to be less civilized had "degenerated" to their primitive state and those peoples who were more civilized had continued to progress from that shared original, civilized

---

8. Marett, *Tylor*; and Burrow, *Evolution and Society*.

9. Tylor makes extensive arguments against cultural degeneration in *Researches into the Early History of Mankind*.

state. Degeneration was caused by war, oppression, forced migration of peoples and "various other causes."[10]

The second stream of the nineteenth-century debate about the origins of "savages" stems from Darwinism. Employing Darwin's evolutionary model in the study of human societies was known as cultural evolution. This theory dominated Tylor's understanding of non-western cultures. Cultural evolutionists such as Tylor argued that all peoples, western peoples included, must have evolved from less civilized societies to more civilized societies. From the perspective of cultural evolution, Tylor believed he could trace the trajectory of human cultural development from aboriginal society to Victorian society. These stages of development from less civilized to more civilized could be tracked in contemporary "primitive people." What is particularly significant for Tylor in relation to Lafitau was that he argued that he could "see" these stages of development, examine them in a living laboratory, so to speak.

Tylor argued that the theory of degeneration could not account for the vast variety of stages of cultural development present in the world. Additionally, he argued that the presence of "survivals" from previous stages of cultural development demonstrated not cultural degeneration but cultural progression. Survivals were evidence of evolution from a previous stage of cultural development and provided the links between stages of cultural development. Tylor wrote that survivals were "processes, customs, opinions, and so forth, which have been carried on by the force of habit into a new state of society different from that in which they had their original home, and they thus remain as proofs and examples of an older condition of culture out of which a newer has evolved."[11] These survivals could be seen easily even in modern culture. "[F]or most of what we call superstition [can be] included within [a] survival, and in this way lies open to the attack of its deadliest enemy, a reasonable explanation."[12] Thus, by tracing these survivals to their roots, as could be seen in a "rude" tribe, Tylor believed he could see the evolution of culture. Through ethnographic and philological analysis, Tylor provided "reasonable explanations" for superstitions

---

10. Ibid., 182. "Among the lower races, degeneration is seen to take place as a result of war, of oppression by other tribes, or expulsion into less favourable situations, and of various other causes."

11. Tylor, *Primitive Culture*, 15.

12. Ibid.

and thereby traced the development of culture back through less developed states in order to demonstrate the trajectory of cultural evolution.

Survivals played an important role in Tylor's theory because they provided the links between the different stages of evolution in diverse cultures. Survivals were the links that connected developmental stages of civilization, showing the shared heritage of human culture. Tylor stated that his goal was "to treat mankind as homogeneous in nature, though placed in different grades of civilization."[13] Survivals were also the key to identifying those different grades of civilization. They pointed the way to the single point of origin from which all human religion (and culture) evolved and allowed Tylor to trace their development over time and space. By comparing survivals, Tylor, a monogenesist, thought he could trace humanity's development back to that original point.[14]

Tylor saw the origin of religion in natural religion. He understood natural religion to be opposed to Revealed Religion. For Tylor natural religion was the source of all religion. Any religion that came after that originary moment contained the root of natural religion even if that religion was lower on the evolutionary scale. Tylor argued that the "modern savage world" more or less represents the "animism of remotely ancient races of mankind."[15] The animism of these modern savages represented an earlier stage of the cultural development of natural religion: "Savage animism, ... expanding to a yet wider doctrine of spiritual beings animating and controlling the universe in all its parts, becomes a theory of personal causes developed into a general philosophy of man and nature. As such, it may be reasonably accounted for as the direct product of 'natural religion.'"[16] Tylor

---

13. Ibid., 6–7.

14. Jean Leopold argues that Tylor's concept of survivals originated with the Grimm Brothers rather than with the Scottish and English Enlightenment, as had been previously argued by George Stocking. Leopold, *Culture*. See also Stocking, *Victorian Anthropology*. "Similarly, although a comprehensive review of Tylor's German readings contributes to our more detailed understanding of his relationship to the German intellectual tradition, it does not change the major outlines. He began in the English empiricist tradition, and after an excursion into German thought—stimulated by his early ethnological interest in comparative philology—he turned again, in the context of the Darwinian debate, to more congenial sources: the Enlightenment and utilitarian traditions, and the contemporary natural sciences, which were dominant intellectual influences on Primitive Culture. In this context, the fundamental opposition between Tylor's characteristic mode of inquiry and another more characteristic of the German tradition becomes clearly evident." (304)

15. Tylor, *Primitive Culture*, 441.

16. Ibid., 442–42. Tylor offers this footnote for natural religion: "Bishop Wilkins 1694

understood natural religion as a religion known through the principles of reason but without revelation. Animism was based on what Tylor called a "doctrine of souls." This doctrine developed from Tylor's general definition of religion as "belief in spirits." At its core, this belief in spirits was the expression of a general philosophy about the nature of the world. Spirits believed to embody trees, mountains, and streams evolved over time into spiritual beings who animated and controlled the entire universe. Tylor argued that as poetry is to modern humanity so was animism to the primitive tribes. Natural religion was the root of savage animism. Yet natural religion was also the height of religious evolution.[17] Religion at its most evolved involved a return to principles of religion without revelation. Natural religion is both the alpha and omega of all religion and its alpha can be seen in primitive animism.

Tylor's theory of religion had a different theological motivation than Lafitau's, though Tylor was still on the same basic path. He, too, was looking for the single point of origin of religion and he, too, was tracing similarities over time and space to demonstrate the religious unity of humankind. He also believed all humans were imbued with religion, that all peoples had some form of religion from the very origin of culture.

In terms of their comparisons, both Lafitau and Tylor find the same origins for religion. In *Religion in Primitive Culture* Tylor writes "No religion of mankind [sic] lies in utter isolation from the rest, and the thoughts and principles of modern Christianity are attached to intellectual clues which run back through far præ-Christian ages to the very origin of human civilization, perhaps even human existence."[18] Both Tylor and Lafitau saw "thoughts and principles of modern Christianity" in pre-Christian civilizations. The search for the roots of Christianity in other cultures connects Tylor and Lafitau. Tylor and Lafitau are united in several presuppositions, not the least of which is a belief in the superiority of Christianity in the history of the development of culture.

Lafitau and Tylor share a core understanding of what constitutes a religion. For Tylor a "minimum definition of religion" is a "belief in

---

'I call that Natural Religion, which men might know, and should be obliged unto, by the meer [sic] principles of Reason, improved by Consideration and Experience, without the help of Revelation']." (441)

17. Tylor's capitalization of this terms follows the pattern that 'natural religion' is the expression of religion throughout cultures and across time and 'Natural Religion' is the height of religious expression.

18. Tylor, *Primitive Culture*, 5.

Work Useful to Religion and the Humanities

Supernatural Beings."[19] For Lafitau, a minimum definition of religion is the belief in an object for "veneration and worship."[20] Lafitau began his book with the observation that religion is necessary for society. In this way he shared with Tylor an understanding of the function of religion. Additionally, Lafitau accepted the analysis that religion was necessary for "political expediency." But Lafitau also suggested a common source for all religions—and that common source is God, "the author of religion," engraved on the hearts of all people—regardless of their proximity to the Old World or the Holy Land. Both Tylor and Lafitau rejected the idea that there are people in the world without a religion. And both Tylor and Lafitau argued that their study brought their readers closer to understanding the roots of religion through an examination of the practices and beliefs of non-western, non-Christian peoples.

Lafitau began with the universal human belief in the soul as the starting point for understanding the development of religion. In a similar vein, Tylor clarified his position. ". . . I have set myself to examine, systematically, among the lower races, the development of Animism; that is to say, the doctrine of souls and other spiritual beings in general."[21] This language of animism may have been foreign to Lafitau but the approach of analyzing the development of belief to understand its connection to other beliefs was not. And where Tylor stated that he would not work out the details of the "problems thus suggested among the philosophies and creeds of Christendom" created by his comparisons with antique cultures, he did spend considerable time speculating on the possible theological origin of native/New World practices.[22] When he speculated on the origin of primitive religion, he found it located in natural religion. Like Lafitau, Tylor begins his theory of the unity of humanity with the contention that the belief in the existence of a soul is a universal human belief that originated at the very start of religious life.

Tylor argued that the belief in a soul is the central belief for the existence of a religion. He found that in "savage religion" there were "consistent and logical" principles rather than a "rubbish-heap of miscellaneous folly."[23]

19. Ibid., 8.
20. Lafitau, *Moeurs*, 92.
21. Tylor, *Religion in Primitive Culture*, 12.
22. Ibid., 11–12. See Tylor's speculation about the origin of native Mexican religion and Catholicism and his conclusions regarding the stratification of cultures to follow.
23. Ibid., 20.

Additionally, Tylor found, in accord with his supposition that natural religion was the root of all religion, that "these principles prove to be essentially rational."[24] Tylor defined animism as including "the belief in souls and in a future state in controlling deities and subordinate spirits, these doctrines practically resulting in some kind of active worship."[25] These rational principles and beliefs were lacking one crucial element, however—the moral element.[26]

Tylor believed that morals were an important part of understanding religion "from a political point of view."[27] The introduction of morals was what Tylor believed separated the religions of the world. He maintained that the greatest power of religion in human society was "divine sanction of ethical laws," and the "theological enforcement of morality."[28] The moral element of religion, however was not universal. The "alliance" between religion and government "belongs almost or wholly to religions above the savage level, not to the earlier and lower creeds."[29] The best the "lower religions" could contribute was a "crude childlike natural philosophy" while those higher faiths used divine law to establish moral standards and duties. These duties provide a public aspect to religion that the lower religions are lacking. The "practical action" of religion in human life was found in the moral contribution of religion.[30]

The public aspect of the moral contribution of religion could be seen in the practice of sacrifice. Exploring Tylor's method of comparison through his understanding of sacrifice will illuminate the similarities between his and Lafitau's methods of comparison and also highlight Tylor's method of using a survival to explain practices in contemporary European culture. Tylor argued that "savage religion can frequently explain doctrines and rites of civilized religion" though he did not think the converse was the case at

24. Ibid.
25. Ibid., 11.
26. Ibid.
27. Ibid., 447.
28. Ibid.
29. Ibid.
30. Tylor makes a clear distinction between "lower religion" as unmoral rather than immoral, however. "Not, [...], that morality is absent from the life the lower races. Without a code of morals, the very existence of the rudest tribe would be impossible; and indeed the moral standards of even savage races are to no small extent well-defined and praiseworthy... The lower animism is not immoral, it is unmoral." Ibid., 446.

all.³¹ By studying survivals, Tylor argued that what was an understandable belief in the "lower culture" was often a "meaningless superstition" in the higher culture. Thus, from Tylor's perspective, it was easy to see that "the development-theory has the upper hand" by tracing from lower cultures to higher cultures.³² The practice or belief he saw in lower culture illuminated the practice or belief in the higher culture. Understanding sacrifice in lower cultures would clarify certain "meaningless superstitions" in higher culture.

Tylor began by discussing different types of sacrifice. The most primitive form was the gift theory or the "offering of morsels or libations at meals."³³ Tylor saw this practice all over the globe and across time. "This ranges from the religion of the North American Indian to that of the classic Greek and the ancient Chinese, and still holds its place in peasant custom in Europe."³⁴ As with many of Tylor's examples, he listed different cultures where he had seen the practice on a scale from most primitive to most advanced. Significantly, he said that the practice could still be seen in contemporary, 'peasant' Europe.

The next step on the developmental ladder in Tylor's understanding of different types of sacrifice was the "abnegation-theory" wherein the worshipper gives "something precious himself" to the deity.³⁵ The strongest examples of this theory Tylor found in the "history of human sacrifice among Semitic nations:"³⁶ "The king of Moab, when the battle was too sore for him, offered up his eldest son for a burnt-offering on the wall. The Phoenicians sacrificed the dearest children to propitiate the angry Gods, they enhanced their value by choosing them of noble families, and there was not wanting among them even the utmost proof that the efficacy of the sacrifice lay in the sacrificer's grievous loss, for they must have for yearly sacrifice only-begotten sons of their parents..."³⁷ Tylor continued to trace the practice into Europe: "Heliogabalus brought the hideous Oriental rite to Italy, choosing for victims to his solar divinity high-born lads throughout the

31. Ibid., 443.
32. Ibid.
33. Ibid., 482.
34. Ibid.
35. Ibid.
36. Ibid., 484.

37. Ibid., 484–85. This example is particularly important because both Acosta and Lafitau used the exact same example in their discussion on the comparison of human sacrifice over time.

land . . . In such ways, slightly within the range of the lower culture, but strongly in the religion of the higher nations, the transition from the gift-theory to the abnegation theory seems to have come about."[38] Through this method, Tylor traced the development of the self-abnegation theory of human sacrifice across time and cultures, identifying the similarities through comparison. Tylor came to the same conclusion as Lafitau regarding the Greek connection to this practice. Just as Lafitau had concluded that the practice of human sacrifice came from cultures that sacrificed prisoners and criminals, so did Tylor. "The Greeks found it sufficient to offer to the Gods criminals or captives . . ."[39]

The next development in the form of sacrifice Tylor found in substitution or sacrifice by effigy. Tylor turned first to Mexico for an example of this practice: "At the yearly festival of the water-Gods and mountain-Gods [in ancient Mexico], certain actual sacrifices of human victims took place in the temples. At the same time, in the houses of the people, there was celebrated an unequivocal but harmless imitation of this bloody rite. They made paste images, adored them, and in due pretence of sacrifice cut them open at the breast, took out their hearts, cut off their heads, divided and devoured their limbs."[40] In this way the common people imitated the human sacrifice performed by their priests at the same festival. Tylor traced this survival over time and space. There was a Greco-Roman equivalent in the substitution model found in the "brazen statues offered for human victims, the cakes of dough or wax in the figure of the beasts for which they were presented as symbolic substitutes."[41] Tylor called it a "compromise" with the Roman desire to keep up the "consecrated rites of ages more barbarous, more bloodthirsty."[42] But was not just the Greco-Roman world and Mexico where Tylor found this particular survival of substitutionary sacrifice. He offered an example from South Africa, that a "Zulu will redeem a lost child from the finder by a bullock" and thereby substitute one sacrifice for another.[43] Substitutionary sacrifice in the form of meal and butter offered in the stead of living creatures was found in India as well, though there the practice of substitution was to "avoid taking life" rather than economy.

38. Ibid.
39. Ibid., 491.
40. Ibid., 481.
41. Ibid.
42. Ibid.
43. Ibid., 489.

Work Useful to Religion and the Humanities

Lastly, Tylor argued the Chinese "work out in the same fanciful way the idea of sacrificial effigy" by using paper figures to serve as attendants for the dead during funeral ceremonies, rather than killing their servants and attendants.[44]

Tylor found that a survival of sacrifice was not absent from "modern Christendom" and substitutionary sacrifice "holds a place in established religion."[45] He gave an account of this survival in Bulgaria, "where sacrifice of live victims is to this day one of the accepted rites of the land."[46] Tylor recounts the rest of the sacrifice in some detail: "sacrifices of lambs, kids, honey, wine, &c., are offered in order that the children of the house may enjoy good health throughout the year. A little child divines by touching one of the three saints' candles to which the offering is to be dedicated; when the choice is thus made, the bystanders each drink a cup of wine saying 'Saint So-and-So, to thee is the offering.' Then they cut the throat of the lamb or smother the bees, and in the evening the whole village assembles to eat the various sacrifices, and the men end the ceremony with the usual drunken bout."[47] Tylor demonstrated the longevity of the survival by tracing sacrifice through time and across the world. However his tone—"the usual drunken bout"—conveyed something about his attitude toward the contemporary practice within 'established religion.' Tylor felt that this survival demonstrated one step on the evolutionary road to evolved, rational natural religion and that he could "see" this evolutionary stage of substitutionary practice in living culture. Even though it was a form of Christianity, it was a less evolved form of religion.

Tylor argued there was yet more evidence of the survival of substitutionary sacrifice in Christianity. That evidence revealed the presence of pre-Christian traditions within Christianity:

> In Christian as in præ-Christian temples, clouds of incense rise as of old. Above all, though *the ceremony of sacrifice did not form an original part of Christian worship*, its prominent place in the ritual was obtained in early centuries. In that Christianity was recruited among nations to whom the conception of sacrifice was among the deepest of religious ideas, and the ceremony of sacrifice among the sincerest efforts of worship, there arose an observance suited

44. Ibid., 481.
45. Ibid., 492.
46. Ibid.
47. Ibid., 493.

to supply the vacant place. This result was obtained not by new introduction, but by transmutation. The solemn eucharistic meal of the primitive Christians in time assumed the name of the sacrifice of the mass, and was adapted to a ceremonial in which an offering of food and drink is set out by a priest on an altar in a temple, and consumed by a priest and worshippers.[48] [my emphasis]

Tylor argued that he had traced the "transmutation" of the idea of sacrifice in Christianity through this survey of sacrifice. Sacrifice was not part of "original" Christianity, it was incorporated from a less evolved stage of religion. Substitutionary sacrifice was not a central part of Christianity, and this led Tylor to a theological question. "The natural conclusion of an ethnographic survey of sacrifice, is to point to the controversy between Protestants and Catholics, . . . on this express question whether sacrifice is or is not a Christian rite."[49] Tylor was uncomfortable with the idea of sacrifice as a central part of Christianity.[50] Through this question, Tylor pointed to a heated issue in the theological debate between Protestants and Catholics.

Tylor concluded this chapter on sacrifice in *Religion in Primitive Culture* with the observation that in general survivals in "the religions of the higher nations have been but scantily outlined in comparison with their rudimentary forms in the lower culture."[51] He does not spend very much time with the problem of Catholicism and Protestantism. He was concerned to express how "the threads of continuity connect the faiths of the lower with the faiths of the higher world"[52] rather than weigh in more than cursorily on the Catholic-Protestant divide. Tylor thought that his survey of the evolution of sacrifice demonstrated the way that his contemporary, higher culture could see the evolution and significance of religious rites "through seeing the meaning, often the widely unlike meaning, which they bore to men of distant ages and countries, representatives of grades of culture far different from his."[53] In other words, the Zulu and the Chinese and the historical Mexica and some modern Christians allowed Tylor and his contemporaries to see the evolution of religion.

48. Ibid., 496, emphasis added.
49. Ibid.
50. See Marett, *Tylor*. In Marett's biography, he mentions Tylor's Quaker heritage but does not say much more about it. Perhaps Tylor's discomfort with the idea of sacrifice in Christianity comes from his Quaker upbringing.
51. Tylor, *Religion in Primitive Culture*. (p. 528)
52. Ibid., 528.
53. Ibid.

Work Useful to Religion and the Humanities

Sacrifice was a key issue for both Lafitau and Tylor. Each used the comparative method, tracing similar elements and "survivals" in order to demonstrate the universality of sacrifice in the practice of religion. Lafitau and Tylor also both thought the universal presence of sacrifice allowed them to observe the practice through different stages of human development, evolution for Tylor, over time. Sacrifice is one of the primary places that both Lafitau and Tylor clearly use the same comparative method to reach similar conclusions.

Tylor wanted to influence his contemporary Christians and hoped that his work demonstrated how his comparative ethnology could help theology. Tylor wrote: "The essential part of the ethnographic method in theology lies in admitting as relevant the compared evidence of religion in all stages of culture. The action of such evidence on theology proper is in this wise, that a vast proportion of doctrines and rites known among mankind [sic] are not to be judged as direct products of the particular religious systems which give them sanction, for they are in fact more or less modified results adopted from previous systems."[54] In other words, religious practice such as sacrifice must be understood from its roots through the contemporary practice. By doing so, the theologian "ought to ascertain its place in the general scheme of religion."[55] This would allow theologians to determine whether the rite is a survival or a new development—a new evolutionary step on the road to natural religion. Tylor concluded that "should the doctrine or rite in question appear to have been transmitted from an earlier to a later stage of religious thought, then it should be tested, like any other point of culture, as to its place in development."[56] Once its place in development has been ascertained, then its general efficacy and usefulness can be determined and the rite can be purged, left behind on the evolutionary path to higher forms of religious practice.

Tylor argued that his concept of survivals provided a method for examining and tracing the development of culture. His comparative method allowed him to see earlier, less developed stages of human evolution.

---

54. Ibid., 537.

55. Ibid.

56. Ibid. As an example, Tylor concluded that substitutionary sacrifice was not original to Christianity but rather a survival of a previous stage of religion. By this method of theological-ethnography Tylor concluded that substitutionary sacrifice could be removed from Christian practice because it belonged to an earlier stage of religious development and as a result, was not efficacious for natural religion, i.e. a Christianity governed by reason.

Leopold argues this is particularly true of *Primitive Culture*: "But Tylor's main interest in evolution in PC was in the evolution of mankind's culture as a whole, from the point of view of Western European man; the doctrine of survivals, he thought, enabled him, as he wished, to see such evolution as historical and actual, though the evidence for it spread through many societies and periods."[57] Tylor "saw" evolution just as Lafitau believed that he was seeing, in living forms, the same kind of cultures has he had seen in reports from other Jesuits and from his antique authors. Both Lafitau and Tylor argued that "savages" provided a window on the way antique peoples had lived and as a result revealed important information about how European life developed and evolved.

Lafitau stated that his work was about "seeking traces of the origin of these people in the dark ages of antiquity."[58] Lafitau created a dialog between antiquity and the lives of Amerindians. This point—that the "savages" were leading Lafitau to understanding ancient authors—shows the strongest connection to Tylor's thought regarding survivals. Lafitau had a dialogical understanding of the of Amerindians he was writing about: when he looked at Amerindians and compared their practices with what he saw in antique texts, he also saw the embodiment of antique practices. He used living Amerindian cultures in order to fill in absent information from antique sources and to clarify points from antique reports. While Tylor's theory is more developed than Lafitau's, Tylor hopes for the same result—to be able to witness the development of religion through survivals and expose superstition to the light of reason, i.e., clarify inherited misunderstanding. This clarification would make religion known through the principles of reason and help religion (and religious practitioners) evolve. Tylor, like Lafitau, thought that by studying the beliefs and practices as well as the physical culture of a people, he could see the evolution of culture.

[M]ISSIONARIES SOMETIMES READ THEIR OWN IDEAS INTO THE RELIGIONS OF THE SAVAGES . . .[59]

Despite all the similarities between Lafitau's and Tylor's comparative methods, there are some significant differences. The most obvious difference is Tylor's use of the idea of evolution. Another, less obvious difference can be

57. Leopold, *Culture*, 53.
58. Lafitau, *Moeurs*, 25.
59. Tylor, "On the Limits."

found in the way that Tylor situated Catholics in his theory of survivals and the evolution of religion. First, Catholics were less developed than Protestants. Tylor argued this could be seen in the ways that indigenous religion and Catholicism were similar. Catholicism demonstrated numerous survivals and allowed for many of the even less evolved indigenous survivals to remain in Christian practice. Secondly, Tylor argued that Catholic missionaries *created* similarities between Christianity and indigenous religion and then later missionaries misrecognized that creation. Where Catholic missionaries saw the enduring providence of God Tylor saw a lack of sophistication in explaining the origin of indigenous religion. Tylor argued that Catholic missionaries created the similarities they saw—in instances such as the development of the "great spirit" to the "Great Spirit"—in order to demonstrate the Christian unity of humanity. Tylor did not need to create such similarities in his theory in order to show human commonality because, Taylor reasoned, survivals demonstrated the connections between different stages of humanity.

Tylor argued that in order to see the evolution of religion, he first had to separate various strata of human civilization on a scale of less civilized to more civilized. Tylor's goal was to identify as the most "primitive" or "rude" race as possible to use as the starting point. Tylor distinguished these strata in this way: "The educated world of Europe and America practically settles a standard by simply placing its own nations at one end of the social series and savage tribes at the other, arranging the rest of mankind between these limits according as they correspond more closely to savage or to cultured life."[60] The criteria that sets any given "nation" closer or further from savage life is based on the "absence or presence, high or low development, of the industrial arts."[61] Tylor further argued that the "implements and vessels" of agriculture and architecture were important, as was "the extent of scientific knowledge."[62] Not to be ignored are the roles of "definiteness of moral principles, the condition of religious belief and ceremony" as well as the structure of social and political organization.[63] Once all these factors were accounted for, Tylor established a "rough scale of civilization."[64] Having balanced his scale, Tylor concluded that "[f]ew would dispute that

60. Tylor, *The Origins of Culture*, 26–27.
61. Ibid., 26
62. Ibid.
63. Ibid., 27
64. Ibid.

the following races are arranged rightly in order of culture: —Australian, Tahitian, Aztec, Chinese, Italian."[65] Notice the presence of Italian at the end of the scale. Italian culture, unlike British culture, was a culture that could be categorized and analyzed according to its location on the civilization continuum below the "European and American" world. In this way, Tylor placed Catholicism below Protestantism on his scale of civilization.[66]

Tylor believed that his moment in civilized development was the highest possible. Historian of anthropology George Stocking makes the following observation about Tylor's understanding of western European civilization, and it is particularly illuminating: "If . . . Tylor saw cultural perfection only at the top of an endless evolutionary ladder, he was on the whole sure that each step of the ladder advanced us toward perfection. The cultural inferiority of those on lower rungs he never seriously doubted. And if he envisioned further progress *in* civilization, his system defined no future *stage*; European civilization was in this sense the goal of all cultural development."[67] Tylor saw Western civilization—with its component pieces, industrialization and Protestantism—as the height of civilization and culture. This is particularly evident in his analysis of various Amerindian practices and their relation to Catholic rituals. Catholics, in Tylor's mind, were not at all far from "savages."

An example of this correlation between savages and Catholics comes from *Anahuac* (1861). This example also shows the nascent stages of Tylor's theory of cultural evolution:

> Up to the present time, there are certain nights when penitents assemble in churches, in total darkness, and kneeling on the pavement, scourge themselves, while a monk in the pulpit screams out fierce exhortations to strike harder . . . A story is told of a skeptical individual who got admission to this ceremony by making great professions of devotion, and did terrific execution on the backs of his kneeling fellow-penitents. Before he began, the place was resounding with doleful cries and groans; . . . The practice of devotional scourging is still kept up in Rome, but in a very mild form, as it appears that the penitents keep their coats on, and only use a kind of miniature cat-o'-nine-tails of thin cord, with a morsel of

---

65. Ibid.

66. Tylor's attitude toward Roman Catholicism can be seen in the example of sacrifice above: "Saint So-and-So, to thee is the offering." *Religion in Primitive Culture*, 493.

67. Stocking, "Matthew Arnold," emphasis original.

lead at the end of each tail, and not such bloodthirsty implements as those we found at Puebla.[68]

Tylor suggested that the roots of this practice were to be found in Egyptian religion and the annual festival of Isis. In this festival, devotees scourged themselves "in memory of the sufferings of Osiris."[69] Regardless of this root of the practice Tylor saw the correlation between Egyptian, Mexican and Roman Catholic religions. This particular practice continued as a survival of a more ancient pagan practice though Tylor found the practice more brutal in Mexico than in Rome.

Tylor was particularly disdainful of the Roman Catholic presence in Mexico. His travels through Mexico, described in detail in the pages of *Anahuac*, reinforced his opinion that Catholicism was not as evolved as his own Protestant traditions: "It seems hard to be always attacking the Roman Catholic clergy, but of one thing we cannot remain in doubt,—that their influence has had more to do than anything else with the doleful ignorance which reigns supreme in Mexico."[70] Tylor was not sparing in his criticism of Catholics and Catholic missionaries. He lamented that the missionaries had not affected native morals. "The religion brought into the country by the Spanish missionaries concerned itself with their belief, and left their morals to shift for themselves, as it does still."[71] From Tylor's perspective, "theological enforcement of morality" was religion's most powerful and important contribution to society.[72] For Catholics to have neglected to enforce morality in indigenous society was a serious failing in Tylor's eyes.

Running through Tylor's works was a two-fold suspicion regarding traditional religion and Catholicism. First, Tylor supposed there must be some common origin to Amerindian/Mexican culture and Roman Catholic Christian culture. In a description of some practices of the Aztecs, Tylor came to a damning conclusion regarding Catholic and indigenous religions. Citing reports of rituals such as children sprinkled with water on their naming day, and a practice called *teoqualo*, translated by Tylor as "the eating of the God," Tylor saw a strong connection between indigenous religion and Catholicism. *Teoqualo* involves Aztec priests baking dough effigies of their Gods and consuming the baked effigies as part of a ritual meal. Rather

68. Tylor, *Anahuac*, 288.
69. Ibid.
70. Ibid., 126.
71. Ibid., 79–80.
72. Tylor, *Religion in Primitive Culture*, 447.

than expressly state this was similar to the Roman Catholic practice of the eucharist, Tylor left that particular conclusion to the reader. Instead he drew less controversial connections. For example, Tylor observed that "the festival of All Souls' Day reminds us of the Aztec feasts of the Dead in the autumn of each year."[73] Based on these similarities Tylor then concluded there must be a connection between ancient Christianity and religion in the New World.

This conclusion is roughly the same conclusion regarding the origin of Amerindian religion as both Acosta and Lafitau presented in their texts. Both Jesuit missionaries shared with Tylor a similar vision of the roots of Amerindian religion, especially regarding connections between Christianity and New World religion. Tylor wrote: "It is difficult to ascribe this *mass of coincidences* to mere chance, and not to see in them *traces of connexion*, more or less remote, with Christians. Perhaps these peculiar rites came, with the Mexican system of astronomy, from Asia; or perhaps the white, bearded men from the East may have brought them"[74] [my emphasis]. Tylor believed there was a common source for Catholic Christianity and Mexican traditional religion. He grounded this assertion in the "mass of coincidences" between Christianity and indigenous religion, as in the example of *teoqualo*.

The second suspicion running through Tylor's thought is that in addition to sharing a common source, traditional religion and Roman Catholicism were virtually the same religion, at least in the minds of the native people: "Practically, there is not much different between the old heathenism and the new Christianity. We may put the dogmas out of the question. They hear them and believe in them devoutly, and do not understand them in the least . . . *The real essence of both religions is the same to them*"[75] [my emphasis]. The implication here is that Tylor painted Catholics with the same brush as "heathens." Rather than bringing morals or significant cultural change, Roman Catholicism put new dogmas over the same practices. The essence, the core of the religion, was the same to the practitioners, whether European or indigenous. Tylor's attitude was that Roman Catholic Christianity barely made a difference in the religious lives of Mexicans and completely failed to touch their morality.

73. Tylor, *Anahuac*, 279–80, emphasis added. Tylor cites Prescott for these examples.
74. Ibid.
75. Ibid., 288–90.

Work Useful to Religion and the Humanities

Tylor clarified what elements of Roman Catholicism and heathenism were shared. He focused on the structure of the religion and the practices rather than the beliefs: "They had Gods, to whom they built temples, and in whose honour they gave offerings, maintained priests, danced and walked in processions—much as they do now, that their divinities might be favourable to them, and give them good crops and success in their enterprises. This is pretty much what their present Christianity consists of."[76] In Tylor's view, especially in terms of practices, Roman Catholic Christianity and indigenous religion blended together perfectly.

Some of Tylor's contemporaries viewed the end of human sacrifice among the Mexica and the Incas as direct result of the presence of Catholic missionaries.[77] Tylor argued that this was not one of Christianity's accomplishments in the New World but rather the result of internal change prior to the arrival of the missionaries in the sixteenth-century: "As a moral influence, working upon the characters of the people, it [Roman Catholic Christianity] seems scarcely to have had the slightest effect, except, as I said, in causing them to leave off human sacrifices, which were probably not an original feature of their worship, but were introduced comparatively at a late time and had already been almost abolished by one king."[78] Christianity did not substantially change the religious lives of the native New World inhabitants. They continued to practice processions and make offerings as they did before the introduction of Christianity. Additionally Christianity's other possible effect, changing the native's moral compass, was not a result of Catholic missionary efforts. Even the great moral affront, human sacrifice, was not affected by the introduction of Christianity.[79]

For Tylor the implications of these connections were that the Catholicism represented a less developed, more primitive stage in the religious development of humanity than natural religion. Unlike the more "rational"

---

76. Ibid., 290.

77. In *Anahuac*, Tylor says of Prescott: "Prescott's Conquest of Mexico has been more read in England than most historical works; and the Mexico of Montezuma has a well-defined idea attached to it." Ibid., 40.

78. Ibid., 288–90.

79. This anti-Catholic thread is obviously missing from Lafitau's work and, while Lafitau does make some comparisons between Catholicism and indigenous religion, he sees Catholicism as a primarily positive moral and ethical influence in the world of the Amerindians. Lafitau saw an exception to this general rule with regard to the alcohol trade (see chapter on Lafitau). Also, the evidence that for possible Christian presence in the New World has completely different meanings for Tylor than it does for the missionary-ethnographers (see chapters 2 and 3).

religion of his own culture, Protestantism, Tylor saw a common irrationality in both Roman Catholicism and indigenous religions. Religious ideas, especially on the "cultured side" of developed civilizations, are eventually replaced by scientific biology or "reasonable belief": "[T]here are many who describe our own time as an unbelieving time, but it is by no means sure that posterity will accept the verdict. No doubt it is a skeptical and a critical time, but then skepticism and criticism are the very conditions for the *attainment of reasonable belief.*"[80] Over time and cultural development, Tylor argued that the ideas of rational religion predominate. Grounded in skepticism and criticism, Tylor suggested religion will evolve to the "reasonable belief" found in natural religion.

Tylor drew on a variety of texts and sources, as well as his own travel experience of Mexico, in order to develop his understanding of the role of survivals in Roman Catholic Christianity and indigenous religion. Tylor took the missionary materials he used almost as field notes.[81] He suspected that missionaries were naively unaware of the work of their predecessors, so unaware they did not recognize it.

Tylor concluded that Catholic Christianity and indigenous religion in the Americas had many elements in common. Tylor recognized that missionaries may have exerted a Christian influence through their missionizing. He maintained that one generation of missionaries may have initially impressed Christianity on a given culture and then subsequent missionaries to the same culture did not recognize the Christian influence of their predecessors. As a result, missionaries saw Christian influence where Tylor believed there was none. In an 1892 article "On the Limits of Savage Religion," Tylor writes: "That foreign travellers and missionaries sometimes read their own ideas into the religions of the savages thus made [sic] require more careful examination than they have yet received ... Especially through missionary influence, since 1500, ideas of dualistic and monotheistic deities, of moral government of the world, and of retribution after death for deeds done in life, have been implanted on native polytheism in various parts of the globe."[82] There are several significant aspects of this quote. First, Tylor makes a careful distinction here regarding "native

80. Tylor, *The Origins of Culture*, 280, emphasis added.

81. The Kingsborough Manuscript is a large collection of Catholic missionary texts and pre-Columbian codices published in England in the 1830s. This manuscript was Tylor's source for much of his information regarding survivals found in Mexico and South America. Kingsborough, *Antiquities of Mexico*.

82. Tylor, "On the Limits," 283–301.

polytheism" and the belief in retribution after death. These "ruder tribes" have been influenced by missionary contact to such an extent that they have incorporated Christian concepts such as a belief in retribution after death into their religion without realizing these are foreign elements.

The "half-civilized Mexican nation" is a prime example of this.[83] Tylor wrote: "it should be pointed out that remarkable Aztec religious formulas collected by Sahagún . . . show traces of Christian admixture in their material, as well as of Christian influence in their style."[84] Tylor was certain that missionaries did not even recognize the degree to which they had influenced these "ruder" tribes. As an example Tylor examined the belief in an afterlife among "ruder" tribes in Australia and North America.[85] He argued that insofar as those tribes possessed a belief in retribution in the next life for acts committed in this life and recognized a unitary God, these tribes had been influenced by Christianity. He maintained that these beliefs were planted in the tribes by visiting (catholic) missionaries.

Tylor argued that by tracing the philological development of the words for "Great Spirit" across the globe he could show the unconscious influence of Catholic missionaries. This in turn would demonstrate the mechanism by which these ideas were planted in an indigenous culture as well as ways that missionaries misrecognized their predecessors influence: "It is only necessary to collect and interpret such divine names for them to be set down to the influence of the missionaries, who for three centuries have been teaching them to the Indians."[86] From Tylor's perspective this teaching has been so prevalent and pervasive that the missionaries do not even recognize their own teachings among the "ruder" tribes.

In rounding out his discussion of missionaries and their failure to recognize their own influence, Tylor wrote the following about Father Filippo Salvatore Gilij, an Italian Jesuit priest who founded and managed a mission

---

83. Tylor, *Religion in Primitive Culture*, 429.

84. Ibid., 430.

85. It is helpful to note that these tribes – in Australia and North America, represent the middle strata of civilization from Tylor's point of view. Tylor's stratum of cultures begin with African tribes as the most " barbaric" in their religious ideas. In fact Tylor argues that the African conception of Heaven is more than likely derived from Christian and Moslem influences rather than actually part of their native African religion. Above the Africans, the North American tribes Tylor considers the "lower ranges of civilization" yet somewhat above the Africans in terms of their understanding of heaven and animism. The middle strata of civilization is represented by the ancient Egyptians. See Tylor, *The Origins of Culture*, 176–91.

86. Tylor, "On the Limits," 288.

The Comparative Method, Religion, and Civilization

in the Middle Orinoco, Brazil.[87] Relating a story about Father Gilij's "discovery" of the indigenous version of the genesis account of Eve's creation from Adam's rib, Tylor writes that this Jesuit missionary was "delighted" to discover the connection between indigenous religion and Christianity: "the kindly but somewhat credulous missionary, though he well knew of European intercourse in the region from 1535 onward, was delighted at this proof of sacred tradition, preserved since the beginning of the human race."[88] This is Tylor's charitable assessment of missionaries and their interactions with indigenous tribes. The missionary took the native account of the creation story at face value as validation of Roman Catholic church doctrine and was (willfully?) ignorant of the history of the church and her agents in the region.

Tylor's less-charitable assessment of missionaries led him to accuse them of creating stories *ex nihilo* or possibly *ex antique-o*. In *Researches in the Early History of Mankind*, Tylor accused a Jesuit missionary of fabricating the existence of an Amerindian tribe that lacked knowledge of fire.[89] Tylor argued that the Jesuit Le Gobien took the story from Pliny. "Pliny places these [fireless] men in his catalogue of monstrous Ethiopian tribes. . . ."[90] Even Pliny was quoting a source rather than describing something he himself had seen.[91] Tylor acknowledged that "the existence of such as a tribe or people would be of the highest interest to the ethnographer . . ."[92] However, Tylor concluded that it was not advisable to give such stories any credence.

---

87. For a detailed discussion of Father Gilij's missionary strategies in eighteenth-century Brazil, see Lourdes Giordani, "Speaking Truth."

88. Tylor, "On the Limits of Savage Religion," 288. Tylor goes on to say that Gilij wrote "Now what have the atheists to say." For Lafitau an atheist is someone who believes that religion is made by humanity and that Lafitau's comparative treatise is organized to demonstrate that all the religion in the world shares one supernatural, non-human source. It appears from this quote that Gilij shared that goal in relating this story. Tylor either does not understand the Jesuit definition of atheism or is uninterested in engaging their discourse. Or it is possible Tylor does not give the "average" missionary credit for being able to construct a system or an argument.

89. Tylor, *Researches*, 232–33. The Jesuit is Charles Le Gobien, author of *Histoire des Isles Marianes* (Paris, 1700).

90. Ibid., 233.

91. "His [Pliny's] mention of the name of Ptolemy Lathyrus shows that he, too, is quoting the voyages attributed to Eudoxus of Cyzicus . . . And with such tenacity does the popular mind hold on to hold stories, that now, after a lapse of some two thousands years, the fireless men and the pygmies are brought by the modern Ethiopians into even closer contact than the pages of Pliny." Ibid.

92. Ibid., 235.

105

He found that these stories "of such tribes have been set up again and again without any sound basis" and that further investigation demonstrated that these peoples do not exist.

Lafitau was not exempt from Tylor's criticism. Tracing the development of the concept of the Great Spirit in North American Indian religion, Tylor focused on how Lafitau's use of capitalization signified a shift in status for the deity, a shift brought about by the missionary's pen rather than indigenous belief: "Let me call attention to passages showing this transition [from a minor spirit to a major deity], when the term 'great Spirit' (the adjective not yet with a capital) is just coming into use as the European equivalent of the Algonquin Kitch Manitu and applying itself to the North American belief in its Europeanized form."[93] Tylor argued that the Amerindians did not have a concept of the 'great Spirit,' let alone the 'Great Spirit,' until after the missionaries transformed various indigenous lower deities into major ones. Lafitau, the remarkable Jesuit of *Religion in Primitive Culture*, while still receiving Tylor's respect, was nonetheless subject to this criticism. Tylor felt that Lafitau was ignorant of the missionizing practices of the Society of Jesus: "Father Lafitau ... shows how the teaching of the Company [Society of Jesus] had consolidated this doctrine during the eighty or ninety years they had been at work. This learned missionary *now simply takes as native belief*, what his own fellow missionaries had recorded their having themselves taught the Indians"[94] [my emphasis]. There are two things interesting about this passage. First, it demonstrates Tylor's strategy for appropriating Lafitau. With regard to Iroquois family structure, Tylor found Lafitau's comparison with the Spartans astute.[95] However, in relation to the Amerindian understanding of God, Lafitau was ignorant of the accomplishments and mission strategies of his order and therefore misrecognized Christian beliefs as native beliefs. On the one hand, missionaries such as Lafitau provided important information for Tylor's inquiry into the evolution of religion and culture. On the other hand, Tylor argued that the information might be tainted by Christian apologetics and that the missionaries themselves were at best credulous and unreliable. Despite the fact that many of Tylor's sources were missionary documents, he had very little respect for the ways that missionaries structured and devised their

93. Tylor, "On the Limits," 285.

94. Ibid.

95. "He even rationally interprets in this way a custom which to us seems fantastic..." Tylor, "American Aspects of Anthropology," 229.

The Comparative Method, Religion, and Civilization

own systems—in some cases, systems very similar to his own. He did not recognize the comparative methods developed by the missionaries he used to develop his own comparative system. Lafitau was very explicit about his "system," but Tylor makes no mention of Lafitau's system or Lafitau's comparisons. By undermining the projects of the missionary-ethnographers (and, in Lafitau's case, missionary-anthropologist), Tylor solidified the differences between his theory and that of the Catholic missionaries.[96]

Tylor continued his critique of Lafitau in another passage. Tylor said that Lafitau "illustrates in the most perfect way, quite without recognizing the bearing of his own words" the crucial mistakes foreigners made when encountering "rude races:"[97] "The whole class of spirits or demons, known to the Caribs of the West Indies by the name of *cemi*, in Algonquin as *manitu*, in Huron as *oki*, he [Lafitau] now spells with capital letters, and converts them each into a Supreme Being . . ."[98] Tylor argued that through the use of capital letters, Lafitau and other missionaries transformed minor deities or spiritual beings into a major, singular deity.

Tylor argued that Catholic missionaries in general, and Lafitau in particular, were so naïve that they misrecognized the work of their colleagues and attributed to the "rude" races a belief that did not exist except insofar as previous missionaries named the deity and the belief for the indigenous peoples. Tylor did not recognize (or purposefully ignored) Lafitau's "system" of comparison. Tylor believed that instead missionaries such as Gilij and Lafitau misrecognized the work of their predecessors and attributed to indigenous religions concepts they did not actually possess.

Tylor argued that for anthropology the immediate challenge of this particular naming and capitalization practice was to identify the origin of each of the names for "Great Spirit" in order to trace its identity in indigenous culture. "Unless the etymology of such names is known, they are not instructive."[99] In order to discover the original spirit, angel or demon, anthropologists must first find the source of the name. Tylor continued that what made missionary influence clear was to "collect and interpret such divine names," in order to separate those that have been taught by

---

96. Tylor, "On American Lot-Games," 55–67. "*This learned observant missionary-anthropologist* [Lafitau] noticed that the American game resembles one brought by the negroes from Africa to the West India Islands" (64).

97. Tylor, "On the Limits," 286.

98. Ibid.

99. Ibid.

the missionaries from those which are authentically from the "beliefs of savages and barbarians."[100] In order for an anthropology of religion to be further developed, Tylor concluded anthropologists must combine the study of language with the study of beliefs to form "a solid foundation on which the anthropological theory of religion must be permanently built."[101] Through philology and the study of religious beliefs, anthropologists could discover the actual origins of indigenous beliefs and separate those beliefs from Christian impositions.

Tylor made this argument because these tribes were very important for his theory of animism. He hoped to lift the veneer of Christian influence off these beliefs in order to demonstrate the way "native polytheism" conformed to his concept of primitive animism: "So far as I can judge, such criticism of accounts of savage theology as has been here employed, while tending to remove as foreign any doctrines approaching the full monotheism and dualism, moral government, and future retribution, *leaves untouched in the religions of the lower races the lower developments of animism*, especially the belief in souls and their continuance after death, names, demons, nature-spirits pervading the world, and reaching their fullest expansion in great polytheistic Gods"[102] [my emphasis]. Tylor hoped to demonstrate that the concept of a monotheistic deity in these tribes, which he had categorized as the most primitive tribes to be found in the world, was a missionary fabrication. By removing the "foreign doctrines," Tylor hoped both to demonstrate the validity of his progressionist vision of culture and to "see" the most primitive form of human animistic, polytheistic religiosity. This was only possible by eliminating the traces of monotheistic Christianity missionaries claimed to have found but actually planted in indigenous religion.

Tylor made use of missionary texts as field notes. Rather than examining Lafitau's own system of comparison to determine how Lafitau (or Gilij, for that matter) interpreted indigenous religions, Tylor used Lafitau's text as raw material for his own theory. In the case of native polytheism especially, Tylor wanted to establish that indigenous religions were inherently polytheistic rather than montheistic. Tylor considered polytheistic religions to be less evolved than monotheistic religions.[103] Tylor used these examples to

100. Ibid.
101. Ibid.
102. Ibid.
103. As a result of this belief, it is possible that Tylor read a great deal of polytheism

demonstrate the lack of sophistication of the Catholic attempts at explaining the origin of indigenous religion. Tylor argued that survivals demonstrated the connections between different stages of religious evolution and demonstrated those connections 'organically,' and opposed a "unity" that, he argued, Catholic missionaries had created themselves.

AN ENLIGHTENED CHRISTIANITY[104]

Tylor was looking for the origin of religion—the same origin that Lafitau sought. Tylor agreed with Lafitau that the answer was found in comparison. Through exhaustive examples, Tylor traced the contours of the evolution of human religion. He did not want to engage in any "direct controversial argument" about the theology that his conclusions implied. He concluded: "In these investigations, however, made rather from an ethnographic than a theological point of view, there has seemed little need of entering into direct controversial argument, which indeed I have taken pains to avoid as far as possible. The connexion which runs through religion, from its rudest forms up to the *status of an enlightened Christianity*, maybe conveniently treated with little recourse to dogmatic theology."[105] "An enlightened Christianity" is a form of Christianity is that closer to natural religion than it is to Roman Catholicism. And as such, it avoids dogmatic theology and doctrinal discussion.

Tylor saw David Hume as one of the most influential sources of "modern opinions as to the development of religion . . ."[106] He believed that Hume provided a method of understanding primitive religion and that Hume's method particularly illuminated the way deities are personified. Hume argued that it is a universal tendency for humans to conceive of beings like themselves and transfer to every object those qualities they find familiar. Tylor found this idea offered a way for anthropologists to conceive of and understand primitive religion. "Our comprehension of the lower stages of mental culture depends much on the thoroughness with which we

---

into his sources, just as he accused the missionaries of reading monotheism into their sources. His emphasis on the inherent polytheism in "primitive" religion was important to his general theory that religion evolved from animism to polytheism and found its most evolved expression in monotheism.

104. Tylor, *The Origins of Culture*, 23.
105. Ibid. *The Origins of Culture*.
106. Tylor, *Religion in Primitive Culture*, 61.

can appreciate this primitive, childlike conception" of creating Gods in our own image.[107] It is the need for this appreciation that Tylor felt would guide anthropology through controversial issues such as the origin of religion and trace it through an enlightened Christianity.

Tylor's method of comparison and theory of the origin of religion is remarkably similar to Lafitau's. While Lafitau believed that God inscribed religion on the hearts of men at the dawn of creation, Tylor believed that natural religion was the root of all further religious expression, however primitive or civilized. He used a comparative method to demonstrate similarities between stages of cultures and to "see" evolution in stories of the past and living people in the present. The two-fold method of comparing survivals to demonstrate the connection between evolutionary stages of religion, combined with the result of "seeing" evolution shows Tylor's similarity to Lafitau.

As Tylor demonstrated the evolution of religion through tracing survivals, he had an aggressive and antagonistic relationship to Roman Catholicism. He used various missionary-ethnographer texts as sources for his comparisons but also carefully positioned Catholicism on the evolutionary scale below Protestantism. Lafitau was in some ways very distinctive for Tylor. Calling him "remarkable," "learned," and, eventually, even "missionary-anthropologist," Tylor recognized the importance of Lafitau and other missionary-ethnographers to his own comparative enterprise. But Tylor argued that Roman Catholic missionaries planted Christian ideas in indigenous culture and then misrecognized those very implantations. Through connecting elements of Roman Catholic practice to more primitive survivals, Tylor believed he had demonstrated the evolutionary distance between Roman Catholic Christianity and an enlightened Christianity. By removing Christian insertions in indigenous religion, Tylor assumed he was on the road toward demonstrating the inherent polytheism in primitive religion.

Tylor treated Roman Catholic missionary texts as primary raw data rather than secondary, interpretive systems. Tylor did not recognize the theological and comparative methods developed by

---

107. Ibid., 62. Tylor quotes Hume: "'There is an universal tendency among mankind to conceive all beings like themselves, and to transfer to every object those qualities with which they are familiarly acquainted, and of which they are intimately conscious ... The *unknown causes*, which continually employ their thought, appearing always in the same aspect, are all apprehended to be the same kind or species. Nor is it long before we ascribe to them thought and reason, and passion, and sometimes every the limbs and figures of men, in order to bring them nearer to a resemblance of ourselves'" (emphasis original).

missionary-ethnographers even while he used to their texts construct his theory of cultural evolution. He argued that Catholic missionaries created the similarities they saw between Christianity and indigenous religion in order to demonstrate the Christian unity of humanity. Tylor did not need to create such similarities in his theory in order to show human commonality. He argued instead that survivals demonstrated the connections between different stages of religious evolution, and demonstrated those connections 'organically,' as opposed to the unity that he argued that Catholic missionaries had created themselves.

5

Conclusion

A comparison of the customs and folkways of the nations could lead us to a knowledge unique in itself...

JOSEPH LAFITAU
Moeurs Des Sauvages Ameriquains

MY STUDY OUTLINES A new approach to the history of comparison in the study of religion by tracing its development from the first moments of contact with the New World in the sixteenth century through the recognized origin of the discipline of anthropology in the nineteenth century. What is new about my argument is that it traces the roots of the practice of the comparative approach to religion back to pre-Enlightenment missionary-ethnographer accounts of contact. The historical trajectory I have outlined suggests the Enlightenment does not mark a sharp break in the understanding of comparative religion. Instead, I offer a vision of continuity over time in the practice of comparison within the study of religion.

Missionaries to the New World made the first steps in the practice of comparative religion. These early missionaries were not exclusively comparativists; they were interested in their own particular goals and the daily life of their respective missions. Bartolomé de Las Casas used comparison of the New World and antiquity in order to facilitate European knowledge and understanding of the Amerindians. He also hoped his work would modify European behavior toward their newly Christianized brothers and

Conclusion

sisters in the New World, particularly the practice of enslaving Amerindians. Bernardino de Sahagún hoped his text would guide future missionaries through the intricacies of the interaction between Christianity and indigenous religion. José de Acosta offered advice for how Europeans could govern New World indigenous peoples justly and what indigenous practices to leave intact in order to ensure the stability of native culture under colonial rule while still converting the indigenous peoples to Christianity. Regardless of their particular mission context, these early comparative efforts show the very beginnings of the method of comparison in the realm of religion.

Following these earliest comparative efforts, Joseph Lafitau added a new twist to the practice of comparative religion. Lafitau examined antiquity in comparison with Amerindians to see the ways those pre-Christian and non-Christian peoples were similar. Lafitau believed the pre-Christian ancients and the non-Christian Amerindians were genealogically connected; he argued Amerindians were the descendents of the Greeks and Romans. As a result, since Amerindians were the descendents of the peoples of antiquity, Lafitau was able to use examples from Amerindian religion and culture to explain antique culture and vice versa. The New World provided a window to European's antique past.

Lafitau argued he demonstrated the unity of humanity through his comparative work. The New World inhabitants were not 'new'—they were relatives of the ancients. He brought a new component to the practice of comparison by using Amerindian culture, belief and practices to observe the ancients rather than using the ancients to explain the Amerindians as his predecessors had done. This is his strongest tie to the "father of comparative anthropology," Edward Burnett Tylor. Tylor argued his comparative approach, through the careful examination of "survivals," also demonstrated the unity of humanity as well as demonstrated human cultural continuity. Tylor's understanding of survivals combined with his comparative approach allowed him to trace the evolution of a belief or practice across cultures and through time. Through a close examination of "rude" tribes, Tylor believed he could witness different stages of cultural evolution. Tylor constructed a comparative model allowed him to "see" evolutionary stages of human religion.

The similarity between Tylor's and Lafitau's models is rooted in their mutual question about culture and religion: what can Amerindian ("primitives" from Tylor's perspective) beliefs and practices tell about Europeans and the origin of religion? From this common ground, Lafitau and Tylor began their studies of the Other. Both Tylor and Lafitau were determined to look for the European past in the practices and beliefs of Amerindians, both were looking for the origin of religion, and both believed they were seeing previous stages of human development.

However, anthropologists and historians of religion have persisted in seeing Tylor's comparative method offering something novel to the intellectual world of the nineteenth-century. When his sources are interrogated by contemporary scholars, they are found to be the usual — the German intellectual tradition and the Enlightenment.[1] But in fact, Tylor was not the first to construct such an understanding of human culture through comparison. His thought is remarkably parallel to the missionary-ethnographers of the Roman Catholic tradition and bears an especially striking similarity to Lafitau's thinking. While Tylor was obviously influenced by Darwin and other intellectual sources, such as the Brothers Grimm, he is also indebted to the work of missionary-ethnographers such as Lafitau.

Tylor's focus was primarily on the evolution of religion and religious practices and beliefs. Tylor was very clear comparative ethnology, especially brought to bear on religious issues, should inform theology rather than destroy theology.[2] In other words, comparative ethnology should guide theology, removing survivals so Natural Religion could break away from superstition and continue to progress. Tylor saw both the root of religion and its highest expression in natural religion and wanted his comparative method to shape the practice of theology to help it evolve further.

Tylor described the various stages achieved by "primitive culture" in order to show Europeans a diagram of their evolutionary history, to map the route to civilization. Lafitau also wanted to understand the path of religious development. Both examined the beliefs and practices of Amerindians in comparison with the ancients in order to see the connections between one stage of culture and another. Both argued these beliefs and practices were important for cultural stability, continuity, and development. Lafitau and Tylor agreed studying Amerindians ("savages") revealed the direction European culture traversed from the beginning of human civilization to their

1. See Leopold. Stocking, *Victorian Anthropology*.

2. See chapter 4. Tylor, *Religion in Primitive Culture*, 537, 161. Stocking argues that Tylor was "suspicious of religion." Where "one might have expected development by 'direct divine communion'" instead there is the rational classification of "the phenomena of culture" arranged "stage by stage in order of probable evolution." See Stocking, *Victorian Anthropology*, 161.

Conclusion

respective moments. Both Lafitau and Tylor believed they could see human history alive and flourishing in indigenous peoples.

For Lafitau, the importance of comparing Christian and non-Christian cultures with what he called "savage religion" was to explain classical history. For Tylor the purpose for comparing survivals in what he called "primitive religion" was to reveal the processes of cultural evolution. He believed he could trace the history of the development of religion from animism to deistic Protestantism through the study of those survivals. Tylor and Lafitau used a similar method and models to construct their theories of the development and growth of religion. Both looked to classical texts and to other missionary documents, particularly those written by missionary-ethnographers such as Las Casas, Sahagún, and Acosta. Tylor's method was enhanced by the use of folklore and Hume's *Natural Religion*, sources not available to Lafitau. Both Lafitau and Tylor employed comparative schemas that used "primitive" people (savages) to "see" the human past. This understanding of "primitive religion" gave Lafitau and Tylor the foundation for their respective theories of the development of human religion. The similarities and differences in their approach to comparison demonstrates a change of emphasis on the role of religion in order to understand Europeans and indigenous peoples. What I have added to the scholarly conversation by delineating the comparative method from Las Casas to Tylor is, following Jonathan Sheehan, a piece of the "story we can tell about religious transformation" in the disciplines of anthropology, ethnology and comparative religion from the sixteenth through the nineteenth centuries.[3]

3. Sheehan.

Bibliography

Acosta, Jose de. *Historia Natural Y Moral De Las Indias*. Translated by Frances M Lopez-Morillas. Edited by Jane E. Mangan, Walter Mignolo, and Frances M. Lopez-Morillas. Durham, NC: Duke University Press, 2002.
Aelian. *Varia Historia*. Translated by N. G. Wilson. Cambridge: Harvard University Press, 1997.
Alden, Dauril. *The Making of an Enterprise: The Society of Jesus in Portugal, Its Empire, and Beyond, 1540-1750*. Stanford: Stanford University Press, 1996.
Alva, Klor de. *The Work of Bernardino de Sahagun: Pioneer Ethnographer of Sixteenth-Century Aztec Mexico*. Edited by Jose Jorge Klor de Alva, H. B. Nicholson, and Eloise Quinones Keber. Austin, TX: Institute for Mesoamerican Studies, distributed by University of Texas Press, 1988.
Augustine, Saint. *City of God*. Peabody, MA: Hendrickson, 1994.
Bangert, William V. *A History of the Society of Jesus*. St. Louis: Institute of Jesuit Sources, 1972.
Bannon, J. F. "Joseph Lafitau." In *New Catholic Encyclopedia*. 2nd ed. Detroit: Gale in association with the Catholic University of America, 2003.
Barthel, Manfred. *The Jesuits: History & Legend of the Society of Jesus*. Translated by Mark Howson. New York: Morrow, 1984.
Boswell, John. *Christianity, Social Tolerance, and Homosexuality: Gay People in Western Europe from the Beginning of the Christian Era to the Fourteenth Century*. Chicago: University of Chicago Press, 1980.
Browne, Walden. *Sahagun and the Transition to Modernity*. Norman: University of Oklahoma Press, 2000.
Burgaleta, Claudio M. *Jose De Acosta, S.J., 1540-1600: His Life and Thought*. Chicago: Jesuit Way, 1999.
Burrow, J. W. *Evolution and Society: A Study in Victorian Social Theory*. London: Cambridge University Press, 1966.
Burton, Richard D. E. *Blood in the City: Violence and Revelation in Paris, 1789-1945*. Ithaca, NY: Cornell University Press, 2001.
———. *Holy Tears, Holy Blood: Women, Catholicism, and the Culture of Suffering in France, 1840-1970*. Ithaca, NY: Cornell University Press, 2004.
Bynum, Caroline Walker. *Wonderful Blood: Theology and Practice in Late Medieval Northern Germany and Beyond*. Philadelphia: University of Pennsylvania Press, 2007.

Bibliography

Cañizares-Esguerra, Jorge. *Puritan Conquistadors: Iberianizing the Atlantic, 1550–1700*. Stanford: Stanford University Press, 2006.

Carheil, Étienne de. "Letter by Reverend Father Étienne de Carheil to Monsieur Louis Hector de Callières, governor, At Michilimakina, the 30th of august, 1702." In *The Jesuit Relations and Allied Documents: Travels and Explorations of the Jesuit Missionaries in New France, 1610-1791*, edited by Reuben Gold Thwaites. New York: Harcourt Brace, 1927.

Carrasco, David. *City of Sacrifice: The Aztec Empire and the Role of Violence in Civilization*. Boston: Beacon, 1999.

———. *Mesoamerica's Classic Heritage: From Teotihuacan to the Aztecs*. Boulder: University Press of Colorado, 2000.

Carroll, Patrick James. *Blacks in Colonial Veracruz: Race, Ethnicity, and Regional Development*. 2nd ed. Austin: University of Texas Press, 2001.

Casanova, José. *Public Religions in the Modern World*. University of Chicago Press, 1994.

Casas, Bartolome de las. *Apologetica Historia Sumaria*. Edited by Edmundo O'Gorman. Mexico City: Universidad Nacional Autonoma de Mexico, 1967.

———. *Bartolome de las Casas: A Selection of His Writings*. Edited by George Sanderlin. New York: Knopf, 1971.

———. *The Devatation of the Indies: A Brief Account*. Translated by Herma Briffault. Baltimore: Johns Hopkins University Press, 1992.

———. "In Defense of Human Sacrifice." In *Bartolome de las Casas: A Selection of His Writings*. Edited by George Sanderlin. New York: Knopf, 1971.

———. *Indian Freedom: The Cause of Bartolomé de las Casas, 1484–1566: A Reader*. Translated by Francis Patrick Sullivan. New York: Knopf, 1995.

———. "The Rationality of the American Indian." In *Bartolomé de las Casas: A Selection of His Writings*. Edited by George Sanderlin. New York: Knopf, 1971.

———. *Witness: Writings of Bartolome de las Casas*. Translated by George Sanderlin. Edited by George William Sanderlin. Maryknoll, NY: Orbis, 1992.

Casas, Bartolome de las, Helen Rand Parish, and Francis Sullivan. *The Only Way*. New York: Paulist, 1992.

Castro, Daniel. *Another Face of Empire: Bartolome de las Casas, Indigenous Rights, and Ecclesiastical Imperialism*. Durham: Duke University Press, 2007.

Castro-Gomez, Santiago. "(Post)Coloniality for Dummies: Latin American Perspectives on Modernity, Coloniality, and the Geopolitics of Knowledge." In *Coloniality at Large: Latin America and the Postcolonial Debate*, edited by Mabel Dussel, Enrique D. Jáuregui, and Carlos A. Moraña, 259–85. Durham: Duke University Press, 2008.

Cavanaugh, William T. "Eucharistic Sacrifice and the Social Imagination in Early Modern Europe." *Journal of Medieval and Early Modern Studies* 31 (2001) 585–605.

Certeau, Michel de. "Writing vs. Time: History and Anthropology in the Works of Lafitau." *Yale French Studies* 59 (1980) 37–64.

Cervantes, Fernando. *The Devil in the New World: The Impact of Diabolism in New Spain*. New Haven: Yale University Press, 1994.

Chakrabarty, Dipesh. *Provincializing Europe: Postcolonial Thought and Historical Difference*. Princeton Studies in Culture/Power/History. Princeton: Princeton University Press, 2000.

Chidester, David. *Savage Systems: Colonialism and Comparative Religion in Southern Africa*. Charlottesville: University Press of Virginia, 1996.

Bibliography

Christensen, Thomas, and Carol Christensen. *The Discovery of America & Other Myths: A New World Reader*. San Francisco: Chronicle Books, 1992.
Clendinnen, Inga. *Ambivalent Conquests: Maya and Spaniard in Yucatan, 1517–1570*. Cambridge Latin American Studies 61. Cambridge: Cambridge University Press, 1987.
Copleston, Frederick Charles. *Aquinas*. Baltimore: Penguin, 1975.
Darnell, Regna. *Readings in the History of Anthropology*. New York: Harper & Row, 1974.
Elliott, John Huxtable. *The Old World and the New, 1492–1650*. Cambridge Studies in Early Modern History. Cambridge: Cambridge University Press, 1970.
———. *Spain and Its World, 1500–1700*. New Haven: Yale University Press, 1989.
Fenton, William Nelson. *The False Faces of the Iroquois*. Norman: University of Oklahoma Press, 1987.
———. *The Great Law and the Longhouse: A Political History of the Iroquois Confederacy*. Norman: University of Oklahoma Press, 1998.
———. *The Iroquois Eagle Dance: An Offshoot of the Calumet Dance*. Washington, DC: U.S. Government Printing Office, 1953.
———. *Masked Medicine Societies of the Iroquois*. Ohsweken, ON: Iroqrafts, 1984.
Gallay, Alan. *The Indian Slave Trade: The Rise of the English Empire in the American South, 1670–1717*. New Haven: Yale University Press, 2002.
Gay, Peter. *The Enlightenment: A Interpretation; the Rise of Modern Paganism*. New York: Knopf, 1966.
Gibson, Charles. *The Black Legend: Anti-Spanish Attitudes in the Old World and the New*. New York: Knopf, 1971.
Giordani, Lourdes. "Speaking Truths or Absurdities: The Religious Dialogues between Father Gilij and His Indian Contemporaries (18th Century, Venezuela)." Online: http://www1.lanic.utexas.edu/project/lasa95/giordani.html.
Greer, Margaret Rich, Walter Mignolo, and Maureen Quilligan. *Rereading the Black Legend the Discourses of Religious and Racial Difference in the Renaissance Empires*. Chicago: University of Chicago Press, 2007.
Grice-Hutchinson, Marjorie. *The School of Salamanca: Readings in Spanish Monetary Theory, 1544–1605*. Oxford: Clarendon, 1952.
Gruzinski, Serge. *The Conquest of Mexico: The Incorporation of Indian Societies into the Western World, 16th–18th Centuries*. Translated by Eileen Corrigan. Cambridge: Blackwell, 1993.
———. *The Mestizo Mind: The Intellectual Dynamics of Colonization and Globalization*. Translated by Deke Dusinberre. New York: Routledge, 2002.
Haddon, Alfred. *History of Anthropology*. London: Watts, 1934.
Hammel, E. A. "The Comparative Method in Anthropological Perspective." *Comparative Studies in Society and History* 22 (1980) 145–55.
Hanke, Lewis. *Aristotle and the American Indians: A Study in Race Prejudice in the Modern World*. Chicago: Regnery, 1959.
Hodgen, Margaret. *Early Anthropology in the Sixteenth and Seventeenth Centuries*. Philadelphia: University of Pennsylvania Press, 1964.
Jacobsen, Jerome. *Educational Foundations of the Jesuits in Sixteenth-Century New Spain*. Berkeley: University of California Press, 1938.
Jaenen, Cornelius J. *Friend and Foe: Aspects of French-Amerindian Cultural Contact in the Sixteenth and Seventeenth Centuries*. New York: Columbia University Press, 1976.

Bibliography

Jesuits. *The Jesuit Relations and Allied Documents: Travels and Explorations of the Jesuit Missionaries in New France, 1610-1791.* Edited by Reuben Gold Thwaites. New York: Harcourt, Brace, 1927.

Kälin, Kaspar. *Indianer und Urvölker Nach Jos. Fr. Lafitau (1681-1746).* Freiburg: Paulus, 1943.

King, C. Richard. *Postcolonial America.* Urbana: University of Illinois Press, 2000.

Kingsborough, Edward King. *Antiquities of Mexico: Comprising Fac-Similes of Ancient Mexican Paintings and Hieroglyphics, Preserved in the Royal Libraries of Paris, Berlin and Dresden, in the Imperial Library of Vienna, in the Vatican Library; in the Borgian Museum at Rome; in the Library of the Institute at Bologna; and in the Bodleian Library at Oxford. Together with the Monuments of New Spain, by M. Dupaix: With Their Respective Scales of Measurement and Accompanying Descriptions.* London: Aglio, 1830-48.

Kluckhohn, Clyde. *Anthropology and the Classics.* Providence, RI: Brown University Press, 1961.

Kristeller, Paul Oskar. *Medieval Aspects of Renaissance Learning; Three Essays.* Translated by Edward P. Mahoney. Durham: Duke University Press, 1974.

Lacouture, Jean. *Jesuits: A Multibiography.* Translated by Jeremy Leggatt. Washington, DC: Counterpoint, 1995.

Lafitau, Joseph-François. *Histoire des Découvertes et Conquestes des Portugais dans le Nouveau Monde.* Paris: Saugrain, 1733.

Lafitau, Joseph-Francois. "Memorial: On the Sale of Liquor to the Savages." In *The Jesuit Relations and Allied Documents: Travels and Explorations of the Jesuit Missionaries in New France, 1610-1791*, edited by Reuben Gold Thwaites. New York: Harcourt Brace, 1927.

———. *Moeurs des Sauvages Ameriquains.* Translated by William N. Fenton and Elizabeth L. Moore. Toronto: Champlain Society, 1974-1977.

Lara, Jaime. *Christian Texts for Aztecs: Art and Liturgy in Colonial Mexico.* Notre Dame: University of Notre Dame Press, 2008.

———. *City, Temple, Stage: Eschatological Architecture and Liturgical Theatrics in New Spain.* Notre Dame: University of Notre Dame Press, 2004.

Leon Portilla, Miguel. *Aztec Thought and Culture: A Study of the Ancient Nahuatl Mind.* Translated by Jack Emory Davis. Norman: University of Oklahoma Press, 1963.

———. *Bernardino De Sahagun, First Anthropologist.* Translated by Mauricio J. Mixco. Norman: University of Oklahoma Press, 2002.

Leopold, Joan. *Culture in Comparative and Evolutionary Perspective.* Berlin: Reimer, 1980.

Lery, Jean de. *History of a Voyage to the Land of Brazil, Otherwise Called America.* Translated by Janet Whatley. Berkeley: University of California Press, 1990.

Lindsay, Lionel. "Joseph Francois Lafitau." In *The Catholic Encyclopedia: An International Work of Reference on the Constitution, Doctrine, Discipline, and History of the Catholic Church*, edited by Charles George Herbermann, Edward A. Pace, Conde Benoist Pallen, Thomas J. Shahan, and John J. Wynne. New York: Appleton, 1907.

Loomba, Ania. *Colonialism-Postcolonialism.* New York: Routledge, 1998.

Magasich-Airola, Jorge Beer Jean-Marc de, and Monica Sandor. *America Magica: When Renaissance Europe Thought It Had Conquered Paradise.* London: Anthem, 2006.

Maltby, William S. *The Black Legend in England; the Development of Anti-Spanish Sentiment, 1558-1660.* Durham: Duke University Press, 1971.

Bibliography

Mancall, Peter C and James H. Merrell. *American Encounters: Natives and Newcomers from European Contact to Indian Removal, 1500-1850*. New York: Routledge, 2000.

Manuel, Frank Edward. *The Eighteenth Century Confronts the Gods*. Cambridge: Harvard University Press, 1959.

Marett, R. R. *Tylor*. London: Chapman & Hall, 1936.

Martin, A. Lynn. *The Jesuit Mind: The Mentality of an Elite in Early Modern France*. Ithaca, NY: Cornell University Press, 1988.

Masuzawa, Tomoko. *The Invention of World Religions, or, How European Universalism Was Preserved in the Language of Pluralism*. University of Chicago Press, 2005.

McCutcheon, Russell. "The Imperial Dynamic in the Study of Religion: Neo-Colonial Practices in an American Discipline." In *Postcolonial America*, edited by C. Richard King, 275-302. Urbana: University of Illinois Press, 2000.

McMahon, Darrin M. *Enemies of the Enlightenment: The French Counter-Enlightenment and the Making of Modernity*. Oxford: Oxford University Press, 2001.

Memoires pour L'histoire des Sciences & des Beaux Arts. Memoires de Trevoux. 4 vols. Paris: Ganeau, 1701-1762.

Mignolo, Walter D. "The Geopolitics of Knowledge and Colonial Difference." In *Coloniality at Large: Latin America and the Postcolonial Debate*, edited by Enrique Dussel Mabel Morana, and Carlos A. Jauregui, 225-58. Durham, NC: Duke University Press, 2008.

Moraña, Mabel Dussel Enrique D. Jáuregui, Carlos A. *Coloniality at Large: Latin America and the Postcolonial Debate*, Latin America Otherwise;. Durham: Duke University Press, 2008.

Morgan, Lewis Henry. *Ancient Society: Or, Researches in the Line of Human Progress from Savagery through Barbarism to Civilization*. Chicago: C. H. Kerr, 1877.

———. *League of the Iroquois*. New York: Corinth Books, 1962.

Morrison, Kenneth M. *The Embattled Northeast: The Elusive Ideal of Alliance in Abenaki-Euramerican Relations*. Berkeley: University of California Press, 1984.

Motsch, Andreas. *Lafitau Et L'émergence Du Discours Ethnographic*. Presses de l'université de Paris-Sorbonne: Septentrion, 2001.

Northeast, Catherine M. *The Parisian Jesuits and the Enlightenment, 1700-1762*. Oxford: Voltaire Foundation, 1991.

O'Gorman, Edmundo. *The Invention of America; an Inquiry into the Historical Nature of the New World and the Meaning of Its History*. Bloomington: Indiana University Press, 1961.

O'Keefe, Cyril B. *Contemporary Reactions to the Enlightenment (1728-1762): A Study of Three Critical Journals, the Jesuit Journal De Trevoux, the Jansenist Nouvelles Ecclesiastiques, and the Secular Journal Des Savants*. Geneva: Slatkine, 1974.

O'Malley, John W. *The First Jesuits*. Cambridge: Harvard University Press, 1993.

———. "Religious Orders of Men." In *Catholicism in Early Modern History: A Guide to Research*, edited by John W. O'Malley, 147-62. St. Louis: Center for Reformation Research, 1988.

Outram, Dorinda. *The Enlightenment*. Cambridge: Cambridge University Press, 1995.

Pagden, Anthony. *European Encounters with the New World from Renaissance to Romanticism*. New Haven: Yale University Press, 1993.

———. *The Fall of Natural Man: The American Indian and the Origins of Comparative Ethnology*. Cambridge: Cambridge University Press, 1982.

Palmer, Colin A. *Slaves of the White God: Blacks in Mexico, 1570-1650*. Cambridge: Harvard University Press, 1976.

Bibliography

Pals, Daniel L. *Seven Theories of Religion*. New York: Oxford University Press, 1996.

Panofsky, Erwin. *Gothic Architecture and Scholasticism*. Latrobe, PA: Archabbey, 1951.

Pardo, Osvaldo F. *The Origins of Mexican Catholicism: Nahua Rituals and Christian Sacraments in Sixteenth-Century Mexico*, History, Languages, and Cultures of the Spanish and Portuguese Worlds. Ann Arbor: University of Michigan Press, 2004.

Parker, Arthur Caswell. *Iroquois Uses of Maize and Other Food Plants*. Ohsweken, ON: Iroqrafts, 1983.

———. *Parker on the Iroquois*. Syracuse NY: Syracuse Univ. Press, 1968.

Parkman, Francis. *France and England in North America*. New York: Literary Classics of the United States, 1983.

———. *The Jesuits in North America*. Boston: Little, Brown, 1963.

———. *Pioneers of France in the New World; France and England in North America*. Boston: Little, Brown, 1927.

Penniman, T. K. *A Hundred Years of Anthropology*. London: Duckworth, 1935.

Phelan, John Leddy. *The Millennial Kingdom of the Franciscans in the New World*. 2nd ed. Berkeley: University of California Press, 1970.

Pomeau, Rene. *La Religion De Voltaire*. Nouvelle edition revue et mise a jour ed. Paris: Nizet, 1969.

Prescott, William Hickling, and John Foster Kirk. *History of the Conquest of Mexico: With a Preliminary View of the Ancient Mexican Civilization, and the Life of the Conqueror, Hernando Cortés*. Philadelphia: Lippincott. 1873.

Richter, Daniel K. *The Ordeal of the Longhouse: The Peoples of the Iroquois League in the Era of European Colonization*. Chapel Hill: Published for the Institute of Early American History and Culture, Williamsburg, Virginia, by the University of North Carolina Press, 1992.

———. "War and Culture." In *American Encounters: Natives and Newcomers from European Contact to Indian Removal, 1500-1850*, edited by Peter C. Mancall and James Hart Merrell. New York: Routledge, 2000.

Rivet, Andre. *The State-Mysteries of the Iesuites, by Way of Questions and Answers. Faithfully Extracted out of Their Owne Writings by Themselues Published. And a Catalogue Prefixed of the Authors Names Which Are Cited in This Booke. Written for a Premonition in These Times Both to the Publike and Particular*. Edited by Peter trans Gosselin, Les Mysteres Des Peres Jesuites. English. London: Printed by George Eld for Nicholas Bourne, 1623.

Rubin, Miri. *Corpus Christi: The Eucharist in Late Medieval Culture*: New York, 1991.

Russell, Jeffrey Burton. *Lucifer, the Devil in the Middle Ages*. Ithaca, NY: Cornell University Press, 1984.

Sahagun, Bernardino de. *Florentine Codex*. Translated by Arthur J. O. Anderson. 2 ed. 15 vols. Santa Fe, NM: School of American Research, 1982.

———. *The Work of Bernardino de Sahagun: Pioneer Ethnographer of Sixteenth-Century Aztec Mexico*. Edited by Jose Jorge Klor de Alva, H. B. Nicholson and Eloise Quinones Keber. Austin, TX: Institute for Mesoamerican Studies, Distributed by University of Texas Press, 1988.

Sahagun, Bernardino de. *Conquest of New Spain: 1585 Revision*. Translated by Howard F. Cline. Edited by S. L. Cline. Salt Lake City: University of Utah Press, 1989.

———. *Historia General de Las Cosas de Nueva Espana: English & Aztec*. Edited by Arthur J. O. Anderson and Charles E. Dibble, Florentine Codex. Salt Lake City: School of University of Utah Press, 1950.

Bibliography

Sayre, Gordon. *Les Sauvages Americains: Representations of Native Americans in French and English Colonial Literature*. Chapel Hill: University of North Carolina Press, 1997.

Sharpe, Eric J. *Comparative Religion: A History*. New York: Scribners, 1975.

Sheehan, Jonathan. "Enlightenment, Religion, and the Enigma of Secularization: A Review Essay." *American Historical Review* 108 (2003) 1061–80.

Smith, Jonathan Z. *Drudgery Divine: On the Comparison of Early Christianities and the Religions of Late Antiquity*. Jordan Lectures in Comparative Religion 14. Chicago: University of Chicago Press, 1990.

———. *Imagining Religion: From Babylon to Jonestown*. Chicago: University of Chicago Press, 1982.

———. "Relating Religion: Essays in the Study of Religion." University of Chicago Press, 2004.

Snow, Dean R. *The Iroquois*. Oxford: Blackwell, 1994.

Starkloff, Carl F., SJ. *Common Testimony: Ethnology and Theology in the Customs of Joseph Lafitau*. St. Louis: Institute of Jesuit Sources, 2002.

Stocking, George W. *After Tylor: British Social Anthropology, 1888–1951*. Madison: University of Wisconsin Press, 1995.

———. *Malinowski, Rivers, Benedict, and Others: Essays on Culture and Personality*. Madison: University of Wisconsin Press, 1986.

———. "Matthew Arnold, E.B. Tylor, and the Uses of Invention." *American Anthropologist* 65 (1963) 783–99.

———. *Race, Culture, and Evolution; Essays in the History of Anthropology*. New York: Free Press, 1968.

———. *Victorian Anthropology*. New York: Free Press, 1987.

Strenski, Ivan. *Contesting Sacrifice: Religion, Nationalism, and Social Thought in France*. Chicago: University of Chicago Press, 2002.

———. *Thinking about Religion: An Historical Introduction to Theories of Religion*. Oxford: Blackwell, 2006.

Tax, Sol. "From Lafitau to Radcliffe-Brown." In *Social Anthropology of North American Tribes: Essays in Social Organization, Law, and Religion*, edited by Fred Eggan. Chicago: University of Chicago Press, 1937.

Taylor, Mark C. *Critical Terms for Religious Studies*. Chicago: University of Chicago Press, 1998.

Teggart, Frederick John. *The Idea of Progress, a Collection of Readings*. Berkeley: University of California Press, 1949.

Thomas Aquinas, Saint. *Introduction to Saint Thomas Aquinas*. Edited by Anton Charles Pegis. New York: Modern Library, 1948.

Thompson, Bard. *Humanists and Reformers: A History of the Renaissance and Reformation*. Grand Rapids: Eerdmans, 1996.

Traboulay, David M. *Columbus and Las Casas: The Conquest and Christianization of America, 1492–1566*. Lanham, MD: University Press of America, 1994.

Tylor, Edward Burnett. "American Aspects of Anthropology." In *Readings in the History of Anthropology*, edited by Regna Darnell, 225–29. New York: Harper & Row, 1884, 1971.

———. *Anahuac; or, Mexico and the Mexicans, Ancient and Modern*. 1861. Reprinted, New York: Bergman, 1970.

Bibliography

———. "On American Lot-Games, as Evidence of Asiatic Intercourse before the Time of Columbus." *Internationales Archiv fur Ethnographie* 9 (1896) 55–67.

———. "On the Limits of Savage Religion." *The Journal of the Anthropological Institute of Great Britain and Ireland* 21 (1892) 283–301.

———. *The Origins of Culture*. Introduction by Paul Radin. Gloucester, MA: Smith, 1970.

———. *Primitive Culture; Researches into the Development of Mythology, Philosophy, Religion, Language, Art, and Custom*. London: Murray, 1920.

———. *Religion in Primitive Culture*. Paul Radin. ed. Gloucester, MA: Smith, 1970.

———. *Researches into the Early History of Mankind and the Development of Civilization*. New York: Holt, 1878.

Voltaire. *The Philosophy of History*. Preface by Thomas Kiernan. New York: Philosophical Library, 1965.

www.ingramcontent.com/pod-product-compliance
Lightning Source LLC
Chambersburg PA
CBHW072156160426
43197CB00012B/2412